ISLAM IN INDIA

The Impact of Civilizations

Edited by
Asghar Ali Engineer

Indian Council for Cultural Relations, New Delhi

SHIPRA

ISBN 81-7541-115-5

Islam in India - The Impact of Civilizations

First Published in India in 2002

Published by :
SHIPRA PUBLICATIONS
115-A, Vikas Marg, Shakarpur,
Delhi-110092 (India)
Ph. : 2458662, 2200954 Fax : 2458662
Email : siprapub@satyam.com.in
Website : www.shiprapublications.com

Laser Typesetting by :
R.S. Prints,
New Delhi

Printed at :
Choudhary Offset
Delhi-110051

Foreword

India is home to the world's second largest Muslim community, a little smaller than that of Indonesia. In the last five decades since independence, Indian Muslims have contributed immensely to the growth of the modern, secular, civilizational state that is India.

This contribution to the body and soul of Indian culture and civilization is easily distinguishable. The Indian Muslim has greatly enriched Indian architecture, literature, the performing and fine arts, crafts, theatre, cinema, cuisine and fashion.

Indian Sufi Music, which is a blend of traditional Bhakti movement poetry and pan Islamic music, is popular in India since the times of Kabir and Amir Khusro. Islamic poetry and songs, which came to India from Iran through Afghanistan, abound in Kashmir and Punjab, each of them home to a strong Sufi tradition, several centuries old. Many indigenous Indian musical instruments like the Santoor, the Shehnai and the Tabla, are evolved forms of ancient Indian instruments with subtle Islamic influences. The '*Saree*', the traditional garment of Indian women, is more often than not, a product of Muslim artisans from Bengal to Banaras, and from Kashmir to Kerala.

This book seeks to articulate these and the many unique influences that the extraordinary creative energy of Indian Muslims has had on our nation.

ICCR had organized an international seminar on "Islam in India: the Impact of Civilizations", in which noted scholars from various countries participated. The papers presented in the seminar have been compiled in this volume.

I am confident that the book would not only be of great interest to scholars in this important area of study, but also to the general public. The articles in the book cover a wide canvas and trace the impact of Islam in India from the medieval to the modern period.

I would also like to compliment Dr. Asghar Ali Engineer for his notable contribution towards making this book a reality, and place ICCR's appreciation for his work on record.

(Suyrakanthi Tripathi)
Director General, ICCR

Contents

Introduction

Asghar Ali Engineer

Islam came into India almost immediately after the death of the Holy Prophet, and some maintain during the life time of the Prophet. What impact did Islam create on Indian life and culture? There are controversial opinions. Most historians and social and religious thinkers feel it had tremendous impact. It enriched Indian culture in all its aspects and also created new institutions. Islam was brought to India not only by invaders through the north but also by Arab traders through Kerala coast.

Along with the invaders through the north many scholars, historians and Sufi saints too came to this country. The popular view is that the Muslims were critical of Hindu religion and considered Hindus as *kafirs*. May be some theologians took such narrow sectarian view; but most of the Muslim scholars, scientists and Sufi saints were greatly attracted by what they saw and studied in India. The Arab scholar Al-Beruni who accompanied Mahmood of Ghazna, was greatly enamoured by Indian religious thought and philosophy. He learnt Sanskrit and mastered the language in order to read Indian religious scriptures like the *Ramayana* and *Mahabharata* in original. He studied these scriptures with great interest and commented on them. It is interesting to note that Al-Beruni was highly critical of Mehmood Ghaznavi demolishing and looting the Somnath temple. He himself was a philosopher and mathematician. He wrote his classical work on India based on his studies of Indian religious and philosophical literature known as *Kitab al-Hind* (The Book of India). He was a critical admirer of the Indian way of life. In his book on India he has quoted original sources like *Samkhya* by Kapila; *Book of Patanjali, Gita i.e.* some parts of the *Bhagvad Gita.* He seems to have used more sources of a similar nature, but he does not quote from them. He has also used the sources of a *Pauranic* kind like *Vishnu Dharma, Vishnu Purana, Matsya-Purana, Vidya-Purana, Aditya-Purana* etc. In the chapter on metrics, a lexicographic work by one Haribhatta, and regarding elephants a "Book of Medicine of Elephants" are also quoted. He also had information on the origin of Jainism, but does not mention his source. Once he quotes Manu's *Dharmasashtra*, but in a manner which makes one doubt whether he took the words directly from the book itself. Some of the quotations which he has taken from these sources are, very extensive, *e.g.* those from the *Bhagvad Gita.* This shows how extensively Al-Beruni had studied the original Indian sources and used them in his work. The advent of Islam in India promoted better understanding by Islamic world of Indian religions and philosophies as well as sciences like medicine and astronomy.

Other Arab scholars were also highly appreciative of India and Indian thought and culture. Abdul Karim Shahrastani, a 12th century scholar of comparative religion also admits that Indians are a great nation and great (religious) community (*umma kabira wa millah 'azimah*) but they have divergent views and ideologies. Also al-Jahiz (d. 869), who was a very talented essayist during the Abbasid period, has praised India for its great achievements. He says:

> The inhabitants of India are highly meritorious in astrology and medicine. They have a peculiar script. In medicine, they have a supreme insight. They have in their possession some strange secrets of the Art of Aesculapius... In making busts and statues, in making pictures out of colours and in architecture they are superb. Their music is also enchanting. One of their musical instruments is known as *kanka* which is played on by striking a chord strung in a gourd... There is an uncommon fund of poetic wealth and oratorical affluence in their possession. They know the arts of medicine, philosophy and ethics. The book *Kalila wa Dimna* (the Arabic translation of the *Panchtantra*) has come down from them. They have plenty of courage and common sense, and many qualities which are wanting even in the Chinese. Cleanliness is a noted feature. They have good looks, tall stature and a taste for perfumes. It is from their land that the peerless ambergris comes for the kings. Streams of higher thinking flowed down from India to Arabia.

Thus we see the early Arab and non-Arab Muslim historians and scholars shower lavish praise on Indians and things Indian. They were all praise for their religion, metaphysics and ethics. Mahmud al-Shabistari, a scholar of the early fourteenth century, in his *Gulshan-e-Raz* even justified idolatry. He says:

> The idol is the expression of love and unity in this world, and to wear the sacred thread is to take the resolve of service. As both faith and unfaith are founded in existence, unity of God is the essence of idol worship. As things are essence of expression, one out of them must at least be the idol. If the Muslims knew what the idol is, then he would not go astray in his faith. The latter did not see in idol anything but external creation, and for this reason he became *kafir* in the eyes of the law. If thou, too, would not see that reality that is hidden in the idol, thou wilt also be not known as a Muslim according to law.

The Sufis also took much from Indian religions, customs and traditions. They invariably adopted local idiom for their discourses which greatly attracted local populace towards them. The attitude of the Sufis towards the Hindus was entirely different from that of the theologians. Theologians were never popular among the masses. They spoke from mind rather than from their heart, the Sufis spoke from their heart. While theologians took narrow theological view the Sufis took liberal humanistic view. The Sufi impact on Indian masses was much greater than the impact of theological Islam.

The Sufis were more interested in the essence and the end rather than the means. Sufi Islam thus easily penetrated among the people who were hardly interested in the theological debates or the *shari'ah* laws. The Sufis, like the *bhakti* saints, represented spiritualism *par excellence.* Thus they found many parallels to the spiritual practices in Islam in the spiritual practices of the *yogis.* The Sufi concept of *fana fi' Allah*, many scholars maintain, also seems to have been derived from the Buddhist concept of *nirvana* which predates it.

As pointed out above, the Sufis never hesitated to adopt local idiom and discourse to put across their ideas to Indian people. A Sufi saint from Maharashtra, Shaykh Muhammad, named his book on Sufism *Yogasangvaha*. He used Marathi language and Sanskrit rather than Arabic terms. He calls *qalb as antahakaran, jalaliyat* as *tamogun* and *kamaliyat* as *sadogun*. In fact he uses all those terms which were used by Patanjali, Shankracharya and the commentators on the Vedantas. And Shaykh Muhammad was not alone or an exception. There were many other Sufis who thought like him. They were genuinely interested in spiritual practices. They knew the outward forms varied but not the content. According to the Sufis, the entire universe is a creation of God and reflects His Glory and all human beings are part of His creation. Most of the Sufis subscribed to the doctrine of *wahdat al-wujud* (Unity of Being) which is quite revolutionary in its implication. According to this doctrine the entire creation is a manifestation of His Glory and hence equally venerable. This demolishes all the barriers between followers of one religion and the other.

It is also important to note that Islam also profoundly influenced Indian thought and philosophy as well as art and architecture. Even temple architecture was influenced by Islamic architecture, not to talk of other secular buildings. There is hardly any field of life in pre-Islamic India which did not experience the impact of Islam. Dr. Tarachand, a great scholar of composite culture in India maintains that Adi Shankracharya's theory of *advaita* (non-dualism) was also propounded under the influence of Islam's most fundamental teaching of *tawhid i.e.* unity of God.

After the advent of Islam in India the Indian culture became a composite culture which is also referred to in Urdu as the *ganga-Jamni tahzib i.e.* the culture which came into existence between the two great rivers of north India, Ganga and Jamuna. Fundamentalists from both the traditions try to ignore this composite culture and put more emphasis on purity of their own tradition. This 'purity' now exists only in certain isolated pockets or in the minds of a few people who swear by it.

As a result of advent of Islam not only cultural but also religious life of India was immensely enriched. Many new religious traditions came into existence. Pranam Panth, Kabir Panth, Sikhism etc, are some of the prominent examples. Guru Nanak, the founder of Sikhism, was greatly influenced by Islam apart from Hinduism. Both Kabir and Nanak worked out syncretic traditions. Besides these there are several little traditions which exist today in India which came into existence as a result of synthesis between Islam and Hinduism.

Urdu, one of the north Indian languages, is also a great example of enrichment of Indian culture due to impact of Islam. Urdu came into existence due to mixing of people of different nationalities in north India — Turkish, Persian, Arabic, and local Indian dialects like *khadi boli* and others. Urdu, like other developed Indian languages, is highly refined and capable of highest literary expressions. It is one of the most beautiful languages of India. Its poetry is extremely rich and combines both Persian and Indian diction and cultural heritage.

Arabic and Persian was spoken by the Muslims who came

from Arabia or Central Asia. Persian became the language of administration both during the Sultanate and the Mughal periods, and being the language of administration it influenced other Indian languages as well. There is no Indian language today either of north or south which does not have several words of Arabic and Persian in it. There are several Arabic and Persian words in Tamil, Malayalam, Marathi, Gujrati, Hindi, Bengali, Kannada and several other languages.

Also, many common practices developed among the Hindus and Muslims. The noted historians like Raychaudhuri and others observe that "One redeeming feature of this period... was the continuity of the process of Hindu-Muslim rapprochement and amicable contact between the members of the two communities, despite the bitter political rivalries of several centuries. Akbar's reign is remarkably important and instructive for the existence of Hindu-Muslim harmony. Illustrations of this are not lacking even in the reign of Aurangzeb. Alawai, a Muhammadan poet, who translated in the seventeenth century the Hindi poem *Padmavat* into Bengali, was the author of several poems on Vaishnava subjects. "Abdullah Khan, one of the Saiyyid brothers, observed the Basant and Holi festivals, and Siraj-ud-daulah and Mir Jafar enjoyed Holi along with their friends and relatives. It is said that on his death-bed Mir Jafar drank a few drops of water poured in libation over the idol of Kiriteswari near Murshidabad. Daulat Rao Sindhia and his officers joined Muharram procession in green dress like Muhammadans. It has been noted by a modern Indian writer on the authority of *Jam-i-Jahan Nama*, a Persian weekly of the early nineteenth century, how Durga Puja was celebrated in Delhi court as late as A.D. 1825."

From all this it can be seen that the impact of Islam on India was immense and far reaching. Coming together of Islam and Hinduism created a new synthesis in social, economic, political, cultural and religious fields. However, some communal and sectarian forces try to continuously undermine the significance of coming together of these two great religions and civilisation. They not only play down its significance but try to promote active hostility between the two by highly selective use of historical resources.

It was, therefore, quite significant that the Indian Council of Cultural Relations thought it fit to hold an international seminar on the Impact of Islam on India. A number of eminent scholars from India as well as from other Islamic countries participated in the seminar which was inaugurated by the then Governor of West Bengal, A.R. Qidwai.

Prof. Abdelhadi Tazi of Morocco presented a paper on the travelogue in India of the Moroccan writer and thinker Ibn Batuta. Ibn Batuta travelled extensively and maintained a diary and recorded all his observations. His writings and notings have become an important source of historiography for that period. He provides us with a wealth of information and his observations—political, social, cultural and religious—are of great interest to historians.

Prof. Abdulhadi Tazi rightly observes that "All facts pertaining to the history of India may be found within the folds of Ibn Batuta's memoirs. The memoirs depict the India of the Middle Ages, highlighting its contribution to building the human civilisation, and shedding light on its social structure as well as political system and its relations with the other kingdoms. Ibn Batuta described India's historical engravings and their significance to the extent that his travels were said to be devoted solely to India and the Sind, and that the rest was a mere preamble or epilogue to his travel to India."

Prof. Tazi also points out, and quite rightly, that "the Moroccan traveller was credited for making India more known not only to the people living on the coast of the Atlantic and the bank of the Mediterranean, but also to all Arabic speakers, indeed to speakers of other modern languages since the memoirs of Ibn Batuta have been translated into as many as twenty foreign languages, including French, English, German and Portuguese." Prof. Tazi even claims that "the reliable information supplied by the Moroccan traveller on India makes him eclipse Marco Polo, the Venetian traveller, because his discerning scholar's mind made him relate news about India without addition or distortion."

Prof. A.Q. Rafiqi from Kashmir University rebuts the often made argument that Islam spread in India at the point of sword. He says, "Islam, contrary to the popular belief, was not forced upon Indians. In fact, there is no evidence to suggest that the Muslim rulers of India engaged themselves in the proselytising activities on a 'mass level or in a fervent, zealous effort to propagate the faith". It would again be a misinterpretation of history to say that the 'Sultanate of Delhi was a theocracy' and that all the resources of the state were meant for the protection and spread of Islam.

Prof. Rafiqi, in his paper "India's Interface with Islam" rightly points out, "In fact it was Sufism which played an important role in the religious and cultural history of India. By the time Muslims established their rule in India, Sufism had reached *modus vivendi* with the so called orthodox Islam, thanks to al-Ghazali, through whose writings Sufism gained a central place in Islam." He further maintains that "Unlike the 'Ulama, the Sufis initiated a movement taking Islam from the classes to the masses. They preached equality, brotherhood, tolerance, respect for human life and devotion to God. They translated spiritual ideals of human love and goodwill into practice and identified religion with the service of humanity." He is also of the view that "Both the Bhakti movement and Sufism stressed what Hinduism and Islam had in common, thereby weakening the contrast in the common mind between the two faiths."

Dr. Indrani Chatterjee discusses in her paper "Slavery and Kingship Among the Indian Gentry in the Late Eighteenth Century". The subject, though rather technical in nature, is of great historical significance in as much as it deals with the rising of slaves in the ruling hierarchies. According to her, the slaves came both from within India and from outside. She says that Sylheti (from Bengal) slaves were found in the Mughal court, and from outside the subcontinent, for example, Turkish male slaves finally ended up in later Mughal Delhi or female slaves of African origin (especially from Abyssinia) found their way into elite households, one of which I have studied, that is the Nizamat of Murshidabad."

It is well-known that Islam gave better status to slaves and many slaves rose to be rulers in India. One of the ruling Muslim dynasties in India is known as the Slave Dynasty. The Turkish slaves became great rulers. Dr. Indrani Chatterjee argues in her paper that the Islamic practices in this respect influenced the Hindu households too. She says, "For example, in Awadh, in many of the Jat and Sikh ruling households of the late 18th and the early 19th century, in some parts of central India and certainly now the evidence is showing that even in the so-called Hindu Brahmanical Peshwai in Maharashtra of the 18th century very similar practices existed."

It is well-known that in Islam children of slave-girls were not considered illegitimate and the slave wives were very much part of the system and they were not considered lower than or lesser than the other wives. This very much influenced the Hindu practice too, as pointed out by Dr. Indrani Chatterjee.

Prof. Akhtarul Wasey in his paper "Indo-Islamic Cultural Interface — A Historical Review" while throwing light on liberalism of Akbar says that Aurangzeb has not been treated fairly by the historians. He says, "Aurangzeb is often held to be a fanatical tyrant but that is pernicious distortion of reality. He may have meted out harsh treatment to his rivals or to the wayward but he hardly ever strayed into a policy of religion-based discrimination. Dara Shikoh was put to death not because, following his grandfather Akbar, he attempted ideological harmony between Hindus and Muslims but because his life threatened Aurangzeb's right to rule."

It is true that Aurangzeb has been much maligned for his anti-Hindu bias and has been portrayed as villain of the piece. Undoubtedly he was orthodox unlike Akbar who was liberal. But that does not mean that he was persecutor of Hindus and demolisher of their temples. The point is that even an orthodox ruler like Aurangzeb was, had to be, considerate towards Hindus.

Prof. Akhtar Wasey further argues, "Had the differences between the two been religious Aurangzeb would not have taken Dara's *munshi* (clerk) into his service and allowed him to pursue the task of discovering inter-religious unity of fundamentals. Hindus continued to hold high positions in Aurangzeb's court and army. He is known to have given grants to various temples."

Akhtarul Wasey also points out "The *sulh-e-kul* (peace with all) approach not only made for stability of rule by Muslim kings but also yielded high quality cultural fruits. Interface of civilisations, especially when they are highly developed, invariably results in a new synthesis without obliterating the distinctive features of either. Islam influenced the existing religions, social customs, architecture, painting, literature as also the political thinking of people."

Khwaja Hasan Nizami Sani who presented a paper "Sufi Tradition and its Impact on Religious Thought", is an inheritor of the great Sufi tradition of one of the greatest Sufi saints of India, Hazrat Nizamuddin Auliya. As pointed out above the Sufis and Bhakti saints were active agents in bringing about cultural synthesis and evolving syncretic traditions of India. They transcended all boundaries and advocated liberal humanism and the doctrine of *sulh-e-kul* (peace with all). The sufis often softened the impact of political harshness of the rulers. Their spiritual guidance brought inner solace to the suffering people.

Hasan Nizami points out in his paper that the Sufis were quite sensitive to the feelings and sensibilities of people around them. They were respecters of other peoples' religious sentiments. This he illustrates with the example of Hameeduddin Nagauri. He points out, "He (Hameeduddin) was stationed at Nagaur, Rajasthan. In Nagaur majority of the local inhabitants were vegetarian. Sufi Hameeduddin after reaching Nagaur made it obligatory for people coming to see him that they should not bring non-vegetarian food with them as it could hurt the feelings of local people. That tradition is still maintained in his eight century old *Khanqah* (hospice). In the *Dargah* of Hazrat Khwaja Moinuddin Chishti even onion and garlic were never used in the official

Langar (public kitchen) utensils, as many Indian sects dislike them also as they dislike meat. It is very interesting to note that the Prophet of Islam himself advised his followers, not to use raw onions and garlic at the time of coming to mosques! perhaps for their smell!"

The Sufi saints more often than not used local language, or even dialects, for their religious and spiritual discourse so as to strike immediate sympathetic cord with the people in the vicinity. Nizami Sani also throws light on this when he says, "Hazrat Khwaja Ajmeri's Khalifa in the third generation, Hazrat Baba Farid started teaching *zikr* or recitation of the name of Allah in local Punjabi-Saraiki language. These things removed all kinds of barriers between the newcomers and the local people. It even opened the gates for exchange of religious knowledge and ideas between them. Hazrat Khwaja Nizamuddin Aulia the well-known scholar and Sufi saint narrates the visit of a lone *Jogi* in the *Khanqah* of his Master Hazrat Baba Farid..."

Coming down to the contemporary period we have numerous contributions by great Islamic thinkers to Indian religious, social and political thought. One of such religious and political thinkers was Maulana Abul Kalam Azad who also actively and enthusiastically participated in the Indian freedom struggle. He wrote commentary on the holy Qur'an which can be included in the classical works on Qur'an from India in the modern times. The Maulana was a creative Islamic thinker who was far above petty religious prejudices.

However, Maulana Azad was also a prolific writer on political affairs during the British period. Prof. Barun De has contributed a paper on 'Two Textual Paradigms of Nationalism in the Middle Period Thought of Maulana Azad".

Prof. De writes, "The 1923 presidential address is only one of a liberal Muslim nationalist's approach to composite Indian nationality. Explicitly Muslim and implicitly Pan-Islamic in its tenor and sympathies (witness his stress on the freedom struggle in West Asia, but not in China where nationalism and incipient socialism were locked in conflict with warlordism... Witness also his critique of *Shuddhi* and *Sangathan* and relative silence about the forces of *Tabligh* and *Tanzim* which were raising their voices in the vacuum created by the defeat of the Khilafat/Sultanate of Turkey..." then he goes on to explain it and says, "This tenor is one of natural bias and not of any failure of relative objectivity. Azad obviously felt that the raising of Hindu communal slogans in the dogdays after the collapse of Khilafat and the outbreaks of mob violence in 1922-23 were greater dangers to India's national movement than minority sentiments which a healthy national struggle could take in its stride."

Prof. De also points out that from the time he edited *al-Hilal* and later *al-Balagh* Azad sought to arouse anti-colonial sentiment on the basis of patriotism alone, leavened by faith in the Quranic tenets and firm love for kin and fatherland. He believed that this alone could bring his people out of subjugation.

D.R. Goyal, an activist for communal harmony and editor of Secular Democracy, a monthly magazine, also lays stress in his paper "Indian Response to Islam" on the composite nature of Indian nationalism after the advent of Islam in India. He writes, "The idea of common nationhood was developed and shared by all Indians irrespective of religious affiliation. Eminent Muslim scholars and divines made a significant contribution to the development of this concept even as they actively participated in the struggle against

British colonialism. Hindus on the other hand, shared the outrage of Muslims when European powers meted out unjust treatment to the Muslim world. Khilafat and non-cooperation movements are outstanding examples of that. So is the consistent Indian support to the Palestine cause."

Islam had a unique experience in the Indian sub-continent. Though it was the religion of the ruling classes for a considerable period of time in Indian history it was also the religion of a minority community unlike Muslim countries where it was a dominant religion. Asghar Ali Engineer, in his paper "Islamic Approaches to Nationhood and Nation Building" deals with this dimension. He points out that Qur'an respects religious pluralism rather than stressing one particular form of worship stresses what the Qur'an calls *istibaq al-khayrat i.e.* excelling each other in virtues and good deeds.

He also refers to the Medinese covenant (*Mithaq-i-Madina*) drawn up by the Prophet (PBUH) with other religious communities of Madina which included Jews and Pagans. The Nationalist Muslims which included the 'Ulama' also, drew on the Prophetic sunnah and legitimised composite nationalism while the separatists among Muslims were talking of Muslims being a separate nation. He refers to Maulana Husain Ahmad Madani's seminal work *Muttahida Qaumiyyat aur Islam* (Composite nationalism and Islam) and says that Islam approves of composite nationalism and there is no rationale for separate nationalism for Muslims. It were modernists among the Muslims, he points out, who talked of separate nationalism which had no religious justification. The noted 'Ulama of the subcontinent, on the other hand, stood for composite nationalism.

Dr. Zeenat Shaukat Ali takes up the issue of the role of Muslim women in the synthesis of Indo-Islamic culture. She discusses the role of many prominent Muslim women; specially from amongst the Mughal rulers. These women had prominent position even in the ruling hierarchies. She says in her paper, "Women played a significant role. Turkan Khatun, Raziya's mother, was the most prominent among Iltutmish's queens. Qazi Minhaj was deeply impressed by her munificence to the 'Ulama, holy men, Sayyids, and Muslim ascetics. Raziya herself not only commanded the army against rebel *iqtadars* but was also a brilliant administrator. Her successors were arch intriguers. *Malika-i-Jahan*, Sultan Nasiruddin's mother, was the principal instrument behind her son's rise to the throne. According to Ziauddin Barani, Jalalu'd Din's wife paved the way for 'Ala'uddin's accession by preventing her elder son from assuming his father's crown immediately after Jalaluddin's assassination."

India's contribution to Islamic sciences, be it the Qur'anic commentary or '*ilm alhadith* or any other branch of Islamic knowledge, has been second to none. It produced great Islamic experts with international reputation. Arabic and Persian flourished during the Muslim rule in India. Prof. Ahmed-el-Sayed el-Heseasi of Ain Shams University of Egypt discusses the contribution of Persian poetry to Islamic sciences from India. Prof. Sayed el-Heseasi points out in his paper that "Due to their love for literature and respect for Islamic culture, Indian kings welcomed poets from Iran. The hostile circumstances back home forced them to come to the courts of Indian kings. Prof. Ahmed deals particularly with the period of Safavid kings in Iran when Persian poetry and literature flourished there; and it was during this period that a number of eminent poets and litterateurs came over to India and richly contributed to the Indo-Islamic culture.

Prof. Ahmed also stresses the role of *bazaar*, coffee houses and public places and their contribution to literature besides the courts. The court poets wrote in expectation of rewards and perhaps, therefore, did not represent people's sentiments. It was poets from public places whose contribution was more authentic. However, there were poets like Khusro who were not only connected with the courts but also freely mixed with the people and genuinely represented people's sentiments. Khusro had this unique distinction.

Like Persian, the Arabic language also had very important place in Indian Islam. The contribution of India in this field is also second to none. Though their mother tongue was not Arabic, most of the Indian 'Ulama, wrote and expressed their views in this language. So while talking of Indian Islam one cannot ignore the role of Arabic language and literature. Prof. S. Ziaul Hasan Nadwi highlights the role of Arabic language and literature in India in his paper. He points out in his paper that, "Arabic language has been an area of interest for Indians since the advent of Islam. And this language was the only medium of conversation and exchange with Arab traders frequently visiting coastal cities of India. Mappilla of Malabar in South West region of India can hardly conceal their Arab origin. Gujarat, Maharashtra, Karnataka and Kerala have been famous centres where Arab traders used to come and stay according to their will."

Prof. Nadwi then goes on to throw light on seminal writings in Arabic on Qur'an, *hadith* etc. from India. It shows how great has been the contribution of Arabic literature from this country.

Thus, these contributions make it very clear that Islam made a great impact on the Indian religious, cultural, architectural and political scene, and both directly and indirectly, Islam, enriched Indian civilisation in ways more than one. Noted historians and scholars have acknowledged the role of Islam in Indian civilisation.

The Role of Ibn Batuta in Writing the History of India

Abdelhadi Tazi

Addressing the history of Moroccan-Indian relations is no difficult task owing to the fact that the Moroccan heritage enshrines a source of paramount importance that broaches the issue under all its aspects to the extent that it constitutes a basic reference for any discussion of these relations.

This source consists of the memoirs of Ibn Batuta, the renowned Moroccan traveller, in which he gives an account of his eight-year sojourn in those lands. During this period, he occupied the senior position of a judge, which gave him an opportunity to gain deeper knowledge about the country. His performance entitled him to an even higher post as he was appointed ambassador of India to China, which helped him round off the picture of India.

By enriching the Arab library with his prolific memoirs on India, this prominent international traveller did not only benefit the Moroccan and Indian culture, but also marked deeply the other cultures since the relations of all parties with India, such as Egypt, Persia and the Arab and non-Arab Iraqi lands, were made known through his memoirs. It is thanks to these memoirs that Egypt, for example, could elucidate the scope of its relations with what was then known as Dahli, and that the state of Persia, strong with its prominent figures and inexhaustible capacity of yore, could fathom the extent of its ties with India, indeed with the Indian leaders.

Travels of Ibn Batuta

Our knowledge of the names, contributions and leverage of the world leaders of that epoch stems from those very memoirs. The memoirs of this traveller were not written for a party to the exclusion of another, but were rather meant for his entire generation, whether in the *Maghreb* or the *Mashreq*, *Al-Sham* or *Al-Hijaz*, Minor Asia or Caucasus, Afghanistan or Turkestan, Andalusia or Sudan.

One conspicuous fact about Ibn Batuta's accounts on India is that they sparked off excessive reactions on the part of his adversaries and rivals who considered his tales to be fictitious testimonies or mere figments of imagination. Ibn Khaldun went so far as to try to elicit an authorisation to prohibit the memoirs, and he might have succeeded had it not been for the action of Ibn Oudrar, the Moroccan premier, who knew about the countries described.

Perhaps it would be interesting for India to note that Ibn Batuta had remained fully loyal to the country during the years he had spent on its soil, grateful to its leaders and scholars, and faithful to the head of state of the time, whom Ibn Batuta continued to praise well after he had left the country. This is a clear example of loyalty, a virtue peculiar to the men who never forget their friends.

All facts pertaining to the history of India may be found

within the folds of Ibn Batuta's memoirs. The memoirs depict India of the Middle Ages, highlighting its contribution to building the human civilisation, and shedding light on its social structure as well as political system and its relations with other kingdoms. Ibn Batuta described India's historical engravings and their significance to the extent that his travels were said to be devoted solely to India and the Sind, and that the rest was a mere preamble or epilogue to his travel to India.

Certainly, some researchers have scrutinised Ibn Batuta and cast doubt on some information he brought about the unknown parts in Asia. But, in the information he told about India they never found any subject for criticism, because he was speaking the way a man would about his home and family.

The Moroccan traveller was credited for making India more known not only to the people living on Atlantic coast and the banks of the Mediterranean, but also to all Arabic-speakers, indeed to speakers of other modern languages since the memoirs of Ibn Batuta have been translated into as many as twenty foreign languages, including French, English, German and Portuguese.

Seemingly, the long passages he devoted to India and the Sind were not sufficient for him as he mentioned once again those countries upon his peregrinations to other sites. He talked about them in Mecca when he was performing the *Umrah* as well as in China, Sudan, Morocco, etc. Wherever he went, there was always someone or something that triggered reminiscences of his stay in India. And when nothing reminded him of India, he would say: "things here are different from India." In his travels, India is mentioned more than seventy times.

The reliable information supplied by the Moroccan traveller on India makes him eclipse Marco Polo, the Venetian traveller, because his discerning scholar's mind made him relate news about India without addition or distortion.

It is quite fortunate to note that the scribe who drafted his travels was faithful in discharging his task. When he wanted to add something of his own; he would warn the reader, opening a parenthesis, unlike Marco Polo's scribe who adopted a different style.

There is a need, therefore, to contemplate some of the passages of Ibn Batuta's travel, which is considered today the most important peregrination in the history of mankind.

Ibn Batuta and his Observations on India

One of the most noticeable facts he related about India of the fourteenth century concerned its political system. He spoke about the informers, who were in charge of giving the Government information about visitors to India, their social status, moral conduct, behaviour, material resources, and duration of stay. The worth of people was gauged according to their work and activity.

It is interesting to note that the Indian leadership had taken a decision prohibiting the use of the term "foreigner" to call the people coming to stay in India. As they considered the term to be derogatory with the hospitality and decorum requirements. They deemed it a duty to change it with a commendatory term, notably the term "dear," which was henceforth used to mean "guests". Furthermore, the protocol placed them before the commanders, a policy which boosted trade transactions and encouraged Khurasani, Iraqi, Shami, Egyptian and Moroccan investors to go to that country.

The pervasive spirit of coexistence prevailing in that country *vis-à-vis* various countries and religions may be equated with what is called today "religious tolerance." The State capitalised on all capacities and skills regardless of colour or religion. Ibn Batuta lived deeply this type of life, which he expressed in a particular style reflecting the reality of the country.

The Moroccan traveller spoke about a very elaborate *national mail* system, functioning according to a well-controlled timing, which attests to the existence of a top-quality institution. On speaking about this institution, he deliberately cited the terminology used, which gives an idea about his ability to retain terms well after hearing them.

Ibn Batuta made it a point to talk, furthermore, about the status of elephants in India, in a way which stimulates curiosity about this magnificent animal whose contribution in all walks of life in past and present-day India are still strongly felt.

The abundant natural resources of India attracted, also, the interest of Ibn Batuta, who set to enumerate their rich varieties.

It is important to note that Ibn Batuta did not speak chiefly of eminent figures, princes and sects with which India was teeming; he spoke also about the administration as well as the local currency which bore different names from today. He compared Indian money with the Moroccan currency, giving highly important economic information. He likewise, talked about India's defence system, describing their swords, catapults, etc. in addition to their river boats which brought together the far-reaching parts of the country, especially the Sind river which carried an array of boats, some of which were reminiscent of Moroccan ships.

Ibn Batuta and Indian Arts

Ibn Batuta did not fail to talk about artists and singers. On his way to the capital, contemplating the relics of the men of yore, manifested in pictures and monuments that bore engravings in the Indian scripts as he said, he spoke about those artists and singers in the way he would about Sufis and religious scholars.

Ibn Batuta's travel represents the best tourist guide which sincerely depicts the spell-binding beauties of India in a way unparalleled in present-day posters and brochures.

Suffice it for the tourist authorities in India to quote him describing an Indian meadow or other sites and events, because he wrote about India in the style of a righteous man, fully loyal to his memories and acquaintances, for he is mindful of the saying: "*God will ask you about your loyalty even to a friend of one hour.*"

As accustomed when Ibn Batuta visited a site, he devoted a lengthy introduction to India, in which he spoke about the customs of certain regions, until he reached *Dahli.* Then he gave a description of this great city, which actually consisted of four towns with their own walls, bastions, infrastructures, markets, including the great mosque, which still exists today, especially its minaret that is considered one of the wonders of the world in view of its size and spacious alleys.

To give an idea about the academic climate of the Capital, he introduced a number of its scholars, before broaching its ancient history and that of its sultans, including the female Sultan Radiya. He did not fail to address the long-standing rivalry between certain leaders to grasp the reins of power, which resulted in a number of tragedies that were a customary phenomenon among politicians. He then spoke about

Sultan Ghiatu Din Tughlaq Shah, father of his friend Sultan Muhammad Shah.

It is also interesting to note his discussion of the phenomenon of astrologers, a widespread phenomenon in any time and place. But when he reached Sultan Muhammad Shah in his discussion, he devoted a full passage of his travels to the description of the royal palace in Delhi, without neglecting its staff, or the customs in force, the order of seating, and the use of elephants as a means of transport by statesmen just as they would ride sumptuous cars today.

His talk about the "great throne" and the "great censer" on the occasion of the Sultan's celebration of the Feast were very interesting. I always tried to find a way to reconstruct in mind that sizable, mobile throne as well as the impressive censer. They were indeed a symbol of power, might, prosperity, and lofty standing.

The first-hand testimonies brought by Ibn Batuta regarding India were indeed exciting, although they were contested by a number of people who charged our traveller with lying. The most exciting pieces of information remain, though, those concerning the acts of compassion or wrath taken by the Sultan *vis-à-vis* people.

At this stage, Ibn Batuta embarks upon a series of daily chronicles, gladdening at times and distressing at others. In both cases, the reader feels that he is a man of principles.

Speaking about the considerable generosity of the Sultan, Ibn Batuta seized the opportunity to mention a historic event, namely the coming of the son of the Abbassid Caliph, Ghiathu Din Muhammad Ben Abdul Qaher Ben Yusuf Ben Abdul Aziz Ben-al-Mustansu bi Allah al-Abbassi al-Baghdadi, who took refuge in Egypt. He related events not existing in any history book other than Ibn Batuta's memoirs.

This event was of interest to the history of India, Baghdad, Egypt and Morocco as well. But why Morocco? Because the son of the Caliph had kept Ahmed, son of Ibn Batuta, without the father knowing anything about the matter, when he entrusted him with the diplomatic mission we mentioned before.

Ibn Batuta finds also an opportunity to talk about a historic event of no lesser importance, when he tells the story of an Arab family having strong political leverage in Al-Sham (Syria). It is the family of Al-Muhanna, Emir of the Arabs of Al-Sham, who are mentioned in every book of history in view of their relation with the Tartars and the Romans. One of the princes from this family happened to come to India. It was Prince Saifu Din, who had married the sister of Sultan Muhammad Bin Tughlaq, and about whom Ibn Batuta tells us many happy and sad events. No matter how hard one tries to summarise the details brought by Ibn Batuta, one still fails. The reader had better read his travels over and over again in order to grasp the facts fully.

The passage in which Ibn Batuta speaks about his meeting with the Sultan on 4 Shuwal 734 A.H. (8 June 1334 A.D.) is immensely gratifying. The Sultan knew about the Moroccan state of Bani Abdul Mu'min, whose reputation had spread far and wide till the Indian continent at the time. When the Sultan realised he had in his presence a man belonging to the Empire of Bani Abdul Mumin in the far west, an empire which stretched from farthest Morocco to the Nile, gnawing lands from Southern Europe, the Sultan's love for that Moroccan increased.

It was, therefore, only natural that he should dispatch this traveller as his ambassador to the Emperor of China, Tuhuan Timor. The importance of the post of Ambassador to China was not ascribed to its vastness, or to the valuable presents it brought, but rather to the fact that it recorded the history of Chinese-Indian relations, indeed the history of the *first contact of Buddhism with Islam.* He described in detail the results of these contacts.

These are a few points about Ibn Batuta's memoirs of India. They make us feel that this man had discharged his duty by endeavouring to grasp its features in order to present them to his world on the other side of the land of Islam and Arabhood. It is fortunate that this heritage should reach the West, whose information about India has been actually supplemented and enriched through this unique international traveller.

It is suggested to Indian Council for Cultural Relations to call certain academic institutions as well as some main geographical sites by the names of Ibn Batuta who contributed to drafting the history of India. Morocco has and is still doing the same. It gave the names of some Indian leaders to a number of public squares and important lecture halls. The Ministry of Cultural Affairs in Morocco erected its headquarters in the Gandhi Square.

We are writing here the current history which will be tasteless if not grounded upon the past history. The nations which overlook their past cannot build up their present, nor aspire for a bright future which we fervently hope will bring full prosperity and comprehensive peace.

India's Interface with Islam

A.Q. Rafiqi

Of all the world's religions, Islam is the most misunderstood and misinterpreted. Vicious distortions of Islam have appeared with alarming frequency during the last one decade. Two subtle rhetorical aberrations further cloud the true perception of Islam. The first is the use of the term "fundamentalist" to describe those who engage in violence. The term is a transmutation from Christian thought where its meaning is well-settled and precise. There it refers to those who "believe in the literal, rather than metaphorical interpretation of the Bible". In Islam, all believers are "fundamentalist", as far as the belief in the basic principles is concerned. I wish I were a "fundamentalist", then a non-Muslim would feel more comfortable and happy in my neighbourhood than in the neighbourhood of his co-religionist. Therefore, to refer to those who commit acts of violence as "fundamentalist" is to insult the whole Muslim Community as also to make a deliberate effort to distort the image of Islam.

The second is the expansive use, especially in the print media, of the term "Muslim" to describe violent acts. Terrorism knows no religious limitations. A few examples are illustrative of its universality and of the double standards used in the media for identifying its perpetrators. The genocide of Bosnian Muslims by the Christians was never labelled by the media as an act of orthodox Christians. Similarly the Irish Republican army, has repeatedly bombed targets not only in Northern Ireland but also in London and elsewhere, but their acts of violence have never been described by the media as Catholic. On the other hand the recent bomb explosions in Kenya and Tanzania were immediately labelled as terrorist acts of "Islamic fundamentalism". We must stop affixing lables because all these acts are politically rather than religiously inspired.

It is very important that we understand Islam in its proper perspective without any predetermined notions and prejudices not only because it is professed by more than a billion people but also because Islam and its civilisation have played a far greater role in the enrichment of the human civilisation than is usually admitted by the modern world.

Islam and its spread

It is a historical fact that Islam did begin in Arabia but then spread rapidly and in less than a century the Arab armies conquered land stretching from the Indus River to France. It was not by any means a case of barbarians bursting into lands with higher cultures destroying priceless treasures, leaving behind them ruins like the Huns and various Germanic tribes, and much later the Mongols. In their expansion the Arabs were unquestionably helped by the people whom they conquered on account of their deep dissatisfaction with the empires to which they belonged. The Muslims proved-more tolerant than the empires they displaced. When the holy. city of Jerusalem was recaptured by the "Crusaders" after four hundred and sixty years of Muslim rule "the oriental Christians regretted the tolerating Government of the Arabian Khalifs". Later when Sultan Salau'd-Din conquered Jerusalem instead of imitating the blood-bath of the "Crusaders"[1], not quite a hundred years earlier gave them the lesson of generosity[2].

The phenomenal success of Islam was not a triumph of "fanaticism over sober and tolerant people" but it was primarily due to its revolutionary significance and its ability to lead the masses out of the hopeless situation created by the decay of antique civilisations, Islam spread peacefully and in some places such as Persia and Central Asia it took several centuries for the majority of people to embrace it.

Although Islam had reached India as early as in the eighth century on the "wings of commerce", but Muslim rule did not become a permanent feature of Indian life until the thirteenth century, with the establishment of the Delhi Sultanate.

Islam, contrary to the popular belief, was not forced upon the people of India by the sword[3]. In fact, there is no evidence to suggest that the Muslim rulers of India engaged themselves in the proselytising activities on a "mass level or in a fervent, zealous effort to propagate the faith". It would again be misinterpretation of history to say that the "Sultanate of Delhi was theocracy" and that all the resources of the state were meant for the protection and spread of Islam. In fact the non-Muslims, in general, enjoyed freedom of worship and, to quote S.R. Sharma, their position was "much better than that of many communities in Europe whose faith differed from that of their rulers"[4]. Even Ziau'd-Din Barni laments that "Muslim kings" in India were tolerant and that the

Hindus were allowed to live with honour and dignity[5]. Professor Mohammad Habib has, on the basis of a minute examination of the contemporary sources, come to the conclusion that the Delhi Sultans "paid lip homage to the Shariat"[6]. The enforcement of the Shari'a was more a principle than an actual practice, only to keep the Ulama in good humour. In fact the majority of the 'Ulama was "utterly materialistic in outlook and opportunist in conduct"[7]. Their personal loyalty was to the rulers and no loyalty to the state and religion.

The Muslim rulers of India were conscious of the fact that the population of the country was predominantly non-Muslim and therefore, concord and reconciliation was a political necessity. Thus they, in general, declined to allow religious considerations to affect their conduct of the state[8]. Moreover, Islam, as rightly pointed out by professor Harbans Mukhiya "really meant different things to different people- to Ala-ud-din Khalji and Muhammad Tughlaq, to Akbar and Aurangzeb, to the Ulama and the Sufi saints, although they all swear by it".[9]

Islam and Sufism

In fact it was Sufism which played an important role in the religious and cultural history of India. By the time Muslims established their rule in India, Sufism had reached 'modus vivendi' with the so called orthodox Islam, thanks to al-Ghazali, through whose writings Sufism gained a central place in Islam.

Unlike the Ulama, the Sufis initiated a movement taking Islam from the classes to the masses. They preached equality, brotherhood, tolerance, respect for human life and devotion to God. They translated spiritual ideals of human love and goodwill into practice and identified religion with the service of humanity.

Within half a century of the establishment of Delhi Sultanate, Baghdad was plundered 'and the last Abbasid Caliph al-Mu'tasim was done to death (1258) by the Mongols. The immediate consequence of the Mongol conquest was that the cultural centres of Islam were "practically wiped off existence" throughout the regions where the Mongols established their sway. India was the only country in the East where Muslims possessed vast resources and thus many 'Ulama, Sufis and men known for their knowledge and eminence came to India and settled here. Thus "Delhi started from the point where Baghdad and Bukhara had left"[10].

It was these spiritual masters, who came to India, wave after wave, who were responsible for spreading Islam peacefully. Many Sufis who came to India established their *khanqahs* in far flung areas and the network of branches, which gradually emerged, helped the dissemination of Islamic spiritual and intellectual values. A careful analysis of the sites of these *khanqahs* would reveal the fact that most of them were established at important Hindu centres[11] and also in the midst of the lower sections of the Indian population who according to al-Beruni were regarded by the upper class Hindus as "*illegitimate children*". They had no access to temples and no sacred text could be heard or read by them. But the *khanqahs* of the Sufis were open to all classes of people and naturally attracted these despised sections of the Indian society to their fold. Even an ardent admirer of ancient Hindu culture like Havell admits that it was the "sociological programme" of Islam which "*won many converts for it in India*"[12]. It was through these men of

God, who were tolerant, pious and peace-loving that the message of Islam spread in India.

Their job was, however, facilitated by the Monist philosophy of Ibn Arabi. The increasing acceptance of Ibn 'Arabi's doctrine of *Wahdatu'l-wujud* among the Sufis was of particular significance in India. It brought Sufi thought close to the Vedanta school of Hindu philosophy, thereby bringing Islam and Hinduism closer together, to a point where the differences between the two faiths were scarcely perceptible to the untutored mind.

Syncretic Movements

Islam in India, during the so called medieval period, was also characterised by what I.H. Qureshi has called "a perilous triumph"[13]. That is, during the fifteenth century there had grown-up in Hinduism a number of syncretic movements. Under the influence of Islam, various religious reformers such as Kabir, Nanak, Chaitanya, Namdeva, and Tukaram had challenged the social concept of caste and had adopted monotheism. The influence of Islam over Hinduism on these various syncretic sects is called, "*perilous*" by Qureshi because in accepting Islamic values, Hinduism was actually showing its "absorptive" capacity once again. But Qureshi forgets that by the time Islam came to India it had become less and less homogeneous both politically and religiously. Its wider and closer contacts with the alien religions, cultures, languages and life styles introduced a type of diversity in the Muslim society. In fact the emphasis on devotion to a personal God and the challenge to caste were the positive influence of Islam on Hinduism. Both the Bhakti movement and Sufism stressed what Hinduism and Islam had in common, thereby weakening the contrast in the common mind between the two faiths[14]. They strived to bring about an integration of emotions inspired by the ideal:[15]

> Learn from the eyes the way to develop unity and oneness. The two eyes are different but their vision is one.

However, Hindu-Muslim relations underwent a great change during the British rule. Never before in Indian history had the antagonism between the two communities been so widespread and acute as it was in the last 25 years of the British rule. It extended down to mass level and manifested itself in frequent outbreaks of violence, riots and killing of innocent people. But the cause of these riots were only superficially religious, and these were engineered by "mischief makers", enjoying political patronage.

Britishers and Hindu-Muslim Relations

Moreover, the British deliberately and consciously did not allow the growth of fellow feeling and goodwill among the various sections of the Indian people. Throughout their rule they articulated an imperial policy of "divide and rule", which ultimately resulted in the partition of the country. Although the division of the country was not the common man's choosing yet the Muslims who willingly chose to stay in India, are generally accused and blamed for it. Even after fifty years of independence Muslims in India face an "atmosphere of suspicion and animosity" and a section of the majority community, although very small in number, consider them an "extranuous element"[16]. Anti-Muslim prejudices and distortions are not only being fabricated but are also perpetrated by vested interests. The following quotations are a sampling of the views of some modern scholars and writers regarding the anti-Muslim prejudice:

> "Both the Muslim Arabs and Turks who brought Islam into India behaved towards the Indian people in a most barbaric manner...and indulged in most heinous type of vandalism. Thir cruelty and harshness towards Indian *Kafirs* knew no bounds...These invaders had not much to contribute in the field of culture"[17].

> "It was one of ceaseless resistance, offered with one relentless heroism; or men, from boys in teens to men with one foot in the grave, flinging away their lives for freedom; of warriors defying the invaders from fortress for months... of women in thousands courting fire to save their honour; of children whose bodies were flung into the wells by their parents so that they might escape slavery; of fresh heroes springing up to take the place of the dead and to break the volume and momentum of the on rushing tide of invasion'[18].

> "Throughout the Sultanate period (1206-1526) a wide gulf separated the two communities and that, to say nothing of enjoyment of any kind of rights and privileges, the very lives and properties of the Hindus were in perpetual danger. If they could not be converted to Islam en masse or butchered in cold blood, it was because of their great numerical superiority and physical strength"[19].

What these modern scholars and writers suggest is that Islam is a religion of war out for extermination of people of another faith, a religion where there is no scope for catholicity and tolerance.

These prevailing notions could be laughed at as ridiculous, were they not so pregnant with harmful consequences. These notions should be combated for the sake of the national cohesion of the Indian people as well as in the interest of historical truth.

However, I do not deny that there are no trouble makers in the Muslim community. But should the whole community suffer as a result of the mischief of a handful of people. The Muslims of India will also have to make a real soul searching and they cannot always blame others for all their ills. There are certain aspects of life where they will have to make some adjustments and bring some change in their attitude. What the Muslims of India need is a fresh introspection and a critical examination of their problems and find realistic solutions to them without being emotional.

If the Muslims of India want to move confidently into the 21st century, they will have to organise themselves not for confrontation, but for co-operation, in the interest of the country, which belongs to them as much as it belongs to any other community or group of people living in India.

References

1. Cf. Amir Ali, S., *A Short History of the Saracens*, (New Delhi, 1981), pp. 327-28.
2. Ibid., p. 356.
3. Cf. Munshi, K.M., *The struggle for Empire*, Foreword, p. XV.
4. Sharma, S.R., *The Religious Policy of the Mughal Emperors*, (Oxford University Press, 1940), p. 8.
5. *Fatawa-i-Jahandari*, English translation, M. Habib and Dr. Afsar Begum, New Delhi, pp. 47-48.

6. Cf. *Political Theory of the Delhi Sultanate*, pp. 136-7.
7. Ibid.
8. Cf. Barni, op. cit.m pp. 34, 44.
9. *Communalism and the Writing of Indian History*, (New Delhi, 1969), p. 25.
10. Cf. Zia u'd-Din Barni, *Tarikh-i-Firuzshahi*, (Calcutta, 1862), p. 27.
11. Shaikh Muin u'd-Din Chisti established his *khanqah* at Ajmer which was "not merely the seat of Chauhan power; it was a religious centre also where thousands of pilgrims assembled from far and near". Nizami, K.A., *Some Aspects of Religion and Politics in India During the Thirteen Century*, (Aligarh, 1961), p. 184. See also Rafiqi, A.Q., *Sufism in Kashmir from the Fourteenth to the Sixteenth Century*, (Delhi, 1971), pp. 212-13.
12. Havell, E.B., *Aryan Rule in India.*
13. *Muslim Community of the Indo-Pakistan Subcontinent*, (The Hague, 1962), Chapter V.
14. Cf. Rafiqi, A.Q., op. cit., pp. 202-8.
15. The shrines of these saints are still the objects of great veneration and elicit devotion both for Hindus and Muslims. They are the symbols of common culture and peaceful co-existence of the Muslims and the Hindus in India.
16. Cf. Balaram, N.E., *Hindutva*: Facts Behind the Facade, (New Delhi, 1993).
17. Balraj Madhok, *Indianisation*, (Delhi), p. 49.
18. Munshi, K.M., *The Struggle for Empire*, Foreword, p. XV.
19. Srivastva, A.L., *Journal of Indian History*, December, 1963, p. 585.

Slavery and Kingship among the Indian Gentry in the Late Eighteenth Century

Indrani Chatterjee

The division between what is called domestic and agricultural slavery is a false one specially inapplicable to the late 18th century in the case of India. Slaves were not confined to some specific tasks. We cannot infer the slave status from the work they did. Specialists particularly those working in inner Africa and in regions we call West Asia and Central Asia have therefore, defined slavery as being a condition of kinlessness at the first instance. This kinlessness was usually the result of capture and/or of war. This is how people became slaves. But this initial phase was often followed by other transactions in human wealth. Slaves were sometimes gifted to win the favour of their superiors; sometimes they were mortgaged for loans and sometimes they were sold particularly in times of crisis like famine. Now the confusion between free children and slave children being sold at such times led to a lot of debate within the Islamic theological traditions from 15th century onwards. In the 18th century, this tradition of debate is very well represented in the writings of Shah Walliullah's successor,

Shah Abdul Aziz and certainly some of the Usūli tracts, that I have seen in the late 19th century, are carrying forward this debate and we can talk about that at another time. In India, at least from the 15th to the 18th century and early part of the 19th century, most slaves were children under the age of 17 and were mainly female children. The male children on being enslaved, they were castrated and hence lost the capacity to become adult males.

Slavery in Muslim India

Slaves came from regions within the sub-continent, (for example, Sylheti slaves were found in Mughal court) and from outside the sub-continent, (for example, Turkish male slaves finally ended up in later Mughal Delhi or female slaves of African origin, especially from Abyssinia) found their way into elite households, one of which I have studied, that is the Nizamat of Murshidabad. The reason I studied the Nizamat was because of its nature as a fulcrum. It was the outpost of the Mughal empire as the Nizamat of Bengal and at the same time, it was the first region where the East India company came to power. The general phenomenon of slavery in Indian history has been relatively under-studied. I am very respectful towards all my teachers and professors from whom I have learnt a lot but very few of them take the issue of slavery right into how the family and the state is simultaneously changed in the 18th century and how slavery does contribute towards this very important change. Most historians of Indian slavery stopped with the Sultanate (that is, by the early fifteenth century latest) but we don't get very much further. In the case of Bengal, I am specifically looking at a formally Shi'ah household (which in English sources, is called the Twelvth Imamia) and within this household, the issue of diversity that people have been discussing earlier is also visible. That is one very important group of people who were formally Shi'ah, conducting very specific sets of prayers and style of worship. At the same time, they also took part in various different kinds of festivals, rituals, practices, gifts to Brahmans at funeral ceremonies, washing of the body in the Ganges. This was a formally Shi'ah household within which various life cycle practices continue a to be fairly local. This simultaneous locality and formality of Islam is very important in the case of Bengal. However, it is this simultaneous formality and locality within the household that makes this particular household fairly representative of general practice. For example, in Awadh, in many of the Jat and Sikh ruling households of the late 18th and early 19th century, in some parts of central India and certainly now, as, the evidence is showing even in the so-called Hindu Brahmanical Peshwai in Maharashtra of the 18th century very similar practices existed.

Slave Wives of Muslim Rulers

Now what are these practices? The one major component of kinship formation that has been at the core of a lot of recent debate and dialogue and conflict, is marriage. In a particular household, the normal and standard feature was that there were two sets of groups from which wives were taken in the 18th century. One was of the same status, the broadly same kin group, elite set from which wives were taken. At the same time, there was another group of children who were brought up early in their lives by the heads of the households, trained in specific ways and constituted another set of wives. This double pattern of acquiring wives was particularly feasible when the East India Company was trying to control succession, inheritance and, by implication, the construction of genealogies of these households. What influenced the East India Company from the early 18th century onwards was of course the desire to control funds, finances and eventually commerce. But the way they went about doing this, from 1770s is well represented in Warren Hastings' efforts to manipulate the Regency of Mani Begam. Hastings' opponents referred to Mani Begam in very derogatory terms, calling her born a slave, a dancing girl by trade and prostitute by profession'. Of course, the issue in such minds was that Mani Begam was supposed not to have been married to Mir Jafar. The importance that English law subsequently put on marriage in the context of slavery both in their own colonies in the West Indies and in the case of large parts of North India was very different from the way these indigenous households discussed slave-incorporation within those households. In the case of English law in the West Indies, for example where many English plantation owners had slaves, the children born of such slaves were not given the same status as children born of their wives of the same-status. It was this system of differentiation that English law tried to implant in the case of India. Particularly in the case of the ruling households of the 18th century, historians suddenly begin to get the notion of children born of slave-women as illegitimate. This is not a word that is part of 18th century Islamic understanding, theological or practical. In fact, as Hodgson and others point out, the status of children or women does not imply anything about slavery or otherwise. Slaves are very much part of the system. They are not lower or lesser than the wives of same status. Once the doctrine of illegitimacy comes in, it is of course expected that those who are categorised as illegitimate will lose out on various claims in terms of property, in terms of living, and in terms of education. The north Indian gentry is not just specific to the Islamic households, the same thing was also happening in the case of the Hindu Bengali households everywhere in Bengal, in Assam, in Coochbehar, Jalpaiguri as well as in Tripura.

What is important is not marriage in the 18th century, not the ceremonial form of marriage, but the status of mother. One who became the mother of a child had enormous fiscal privileges, had greater potential for incorporation into systems of power as well as into systems of kinship particularly when the son became the Nazim, or became a politically important official. The mother became subsequently raised in status. What her origin was, whether she was bought as a five year old in upper Hindustan as in case of Mani Begum or whether she was herself born of a slave, dancing girl and then incorporated, these were not important considerations where the indigenous household was concerned. However, there were great conflicts also within these kinds of households which I do not want to minimise. The conflicts came about because of the same status wives who also existed. If you look at the chronological pattern of such households, you find that the slave-wives gave birth to children earlier than the husbands acquired what we call 'isogamous' wives, that is, same-status wives. And because the same-status wives happened also to be new, there were great distances between the spouses. In addition, the slave-wife's children were better controlled by the matriarchs, the elder regents of the same households. Therefore, the matriarchs and the slave wives worked hand in hand, sometimes against the homogenous or the isogamous wives' interests. So, there were conflicts. The East India Company, in the name of implanting Islamic law, implanted what is rightly called 'Anglo-Islamic Law'. For the first time, we start getting doctrines of illegitimacy, we start getting tests of marriage whether there is a *nikahnama* or not, what kind of ritual is followed in the *nikah*, whether there were the two witnesses etc.

What we get at the end of the 19th century is a completely re-ordered personal law which is supposed to be Islamic but which has none of the practices of such households which incorporate people and give them status.

Indo-Islamic Cultural Interface

Akhtarul Wasey

Interaction of Islamic civilisation with pre-Islamic civilisation of India goes back to the period when the Prophet brought the message to the Arabs. It is a long and chequered history. The nature of this interface has been changing with time and place as also the level at which the interface took place. There has been a lot of give and take between the two, the process having been marked by ups and downs with change in circumstances in which the commerce in civilizational values was carried on. The end result is that a large segment of the population in the Indian sub-continent follows the faith bequeathed by the Prophet (PBUH). If the entire population of the sub-continent is taken into consideration it is the largest Muslim community in the world, representing all shades and nuances of Islam. Even after the emergence of Pakistan and Bangladesh, the Indian Muslim community is the second largest group, after Indonesia. And be it remembered that the message of Islam to that Indian Ocean archipelago was carried via India, indeed from the Indian soil.

The unique aspect of this interaction is that neither of the two interacting civilisations has been obliterated as happened elsewhere. While in Central and West Asia, North Africa, Malaysia and Indonesia pre-Islamic civilisations have been subsumed into Islam, it has not happened here. Nor has the European phenomena been repeated where the resurgent Islam of the early period swept across that continent but was subsequently swept out. This is no place to go into the reasons behind these phenomenon. What is sought to be highlighted by this comparison is that the interaction here has been more in the nature of coexistence rather than confrontation. And from that has emerged a concept in Islamic thought unknown elsewhere the concept of *sulh-e-kul'*, peace with all. The black-and-white division of the world into *dar-ul-Islam* and *dar-ul-Harb* developed in the circumstances of hostile confrontation have been replaced here by the concept of *dar-ul-Amn* or *dar-ul-sulh*, the region of peace, of peaceful coexistence with those who do not accept the faith of 'Mohammad but follow other creeds and beliefs.

Entry of Islam in India

How and why this happened leads us to the circumstances in which the Islamic civilisation found entry into this region. There have been four major entry points - Kerala, Bengal, Sindh and N.W.F.P. (North West Frontier Provinces). While in the first two instances the carriers of the message were traders in the latter two cases it came alongwith conquering armies. In both cases, however, the spread of Islam was the result of the efforts of Sufi missionaries. There is hardly any evidence of force as instrument of conversion, at least not of its direct use. Probably the need for it was not felt by the protagonists of Islam.

Coastal areas of the sub-continent were frequented for centuries by Arab traders who carried the produce of the region, as also of the Malaysian-Indonesian region, to Europe. Influenced by the preachings of Prophet Mohammad they had converted to Islam with its message of peace, justice and human equality which became attributes of their trade dealings. The people among whom they operated were smarting under the oppressively rigid caste system. The oppressed among them found the social equality of Islam a safe haven from this oppression. Equal opportunities to offer prayers in the mosque stood in sharp contrast to the denial of entry to temples for the lower castes who converted to Islam in large numbers. The rulers of the region also saw these Arab traders as agents of material prosperity and gave them facilities to construct mosques, *madrassas* and *khanqahs.* Some of them themselves adopted the new religion.

In Kerala Islam was brought by traders, not conquerors. They were given all facilities to practise their newly acquired faith by the local rulers. The social equality they observed was in sharp contrast to the social discrimination which characterised the prevalent indigenous tradition. The upper caste Namboodiri Brahmins and Nairs treated the lower castes as untouchables who were not allowed temple entry or equality in social life. The Muslims, on the other hand, prayed together in the mosques, the high and low standing together. This religion of equality and justice became a natural attraction requiring no effort for its propagation or proselytisation.

Another section that had adopted Islam were those Arab sailors who had settled in Kerala and had endeared themselves to the rulers on account of their bravery and loyalty. They were called Mapillas, the dear boys; and they contributed an important element for satisfying the territorial ambitions of the rulers. Therefore not only was no objection raised to their adoption of the new religion but the rulers themselves also felt attracted or impelled to follow them. It is said that Raja Cherman Perumal had invited a Ceylon-bound group of Muslim Arabs to his court and was so impressed by their views that he quietly converted to Islam and requested the group to take him with them to meet Prophet Mohammad and his companions. He entrusted his kingdom to his ministers and accompanied the returning Arabs. He however could not reach the city of Medina and was caught by illness which proved fatal. Before breathing his last he advised his attendants to go back and facilitate the propagation of Islam which they did. Although the date of his journey is doubtful but his contribution to propagation of Islam is beyond question.

So far as the entry of Islam in the conqueror's trail is concerned it was confined to the northern regions. The conquerors of Sindh were Arabs who evinced deep interest in the various branches of knowledge like mathematics, medicine and philosophy. They endeared Islam to people with their sense of justice and equality. Through the Khyber pass came the Pathan and Turko-Mughal conquerors most of whom showed more interest in establishing stable kingdoms than in proselytisation. It was not difficult for them to realise that the aim could be realised better by adopting inoffensive attitude in matters of religion. Even the most pious and devoted of these rulers did not accept the advice, if and when, given by enthusiastic proselytisers, to exercise bias in favour of Islam. Most scholars are of the opinion that if they had not adopted that policy Muslim rule would not have lasted on this soil as long as it did.

Islam in North India

In northern India, as pointed out above, Islam had come in the wake of military conquest of the region by the Turks and Mughals. They refrained from using state power to force Islam because that was in conflict with their political interests. The Turks were engaged in military conflict on one side with Rajput chieftains and on the other with Mongols who had penetrated deep into western Punjab. For them winning the support of the local population was more important than converting it to Islam or bringing it under *shariat* law which would have inevitably led to a conflict. Sultan Balban, when pressed by *ulema* to enforce *shariat*, replied: 'I am as much a Mussalman as the *ulema* but caution dictates against it'. That exemplifies the attitude of the Muslim rulers towards Islamisation.

The same policy was pursued by the Mughals. The advice that Babar, the founder of the Mughal empire, bequeathed to his son Humayun is worth noting in this context. The bequest reads:

1. "Do not allow religious fanaticism to affect your thinking. Do justice without bias. Be respectful to the rites, rituals and beliefs of the people of different faiths."
2. "Avoid cow-slaughter in particular. That will stand in good stead to win over the people of Hindostan and you will bind the people of this land to yourself by the thread of gratitude."
3. "Never destroy and desecrate the place of worship of any religion and always do justice so that the

relationship between the ruler and the ruled may be cordial. That will ensure peace and tranquillity in the land."

4. "Propagation of Islam will be better served by love than by oppression and force."

5. "Pay due attention to different characteristics of your subjects just as you care for differences of weather in a year so that the body-politic may remain free from disease."

And the advice concludes with the exhortation: "My son, India is the abode of people following different faiths and therefore be grateful to the God Almighty who had bestowed upon you this kingdom."

That advice remained the guiding principle of the Mughal policy. It found radical expression in the conduct of Akbar who not only removed all discriminating laws against Hindus, giving them the same rights as citizens as were enjoyed by the Muslims. *Jizia*, the tax levied on those non-Muslims who were exempted from military duty, was abolished and Hindus were given prominent positions in the Mughal armed forces. There was no obstruction to temple construction or observance of Hindu rites and rituals. He encouraged harmonious commingling of the two faiths by what may be called entering into matrimonial relationship with Hindu Rajputs. This practice continued after him so that, in the words of Dr. Mohammad Omar "by the time of Bahadur Shah more Indian blood ran in the veins of Indian Mughals and Muslims than the blood of Iran and Turan and they entirely wore the local socio-cultural complexion."

Akbar also enthusiastically participated in Hindu festivals which were celebrated in full regality in his court. Following that practice common Muslims also took to celebrating Hindu festivals, and even adopted or copied Hindu rites and rituals. Muslims were encouraged to study and understand Hindu scriptures. To facilitate this he ordered translation of important Sanskrit books like *Atharva Veda, Mahabharat* and *Ramayana* into Persian. It is noteworthy that Abdur Rahim Khan-e-Khanaan, a noble of Akbar's court, was a friend of Tulsidas and admirer of Ram Chandra, the hero of *Ramayana.*

Aurangzeb and Distortion of History

Akbar had issued an edict: "In a country under one ruler it is bad that the subjects should be disunited and in conflict with one another... We should therefore string them together in such a way that unity informs all diversity so that each community may continue to benefit from the positive values from its faith and at the same time adopt what is good in other faiths. That would be real praise to and worship of God, and would bring peace to people and order in the country". This may well be described as the manifesto of the *Sulhe Kul.*

Aurangzeb is often held to be a fanatical tyrant but that is a pernicious distortion of reality. He may have meted out harsh treatment to his rivals or to the wayward but he hardly ever strayed into a policy of religion-based discrimination. Dara Shikoh was put to death not because, following his great grandfather Akbar, he attempted ideological harmony between Hindus and Muslims but because his life threatened Aurangzeb's right to rule. Had the differences between the two been religious Aurangzeb would not have taken Dara's *munshi* (clerk) into his service and allowed him to pursue the task of discovering inter-religious unity of fundamentals. Hindus continued to hold high positions in Aurangzeb's court and army. He is known to have given grants to various temples. An order he sent to the governor of Benares reflects his true attitude and policy. The order reads: "Some misguided people oppress and terrorise the people of Benares town and its suburbs and obstruct the guards and priests of its temples in performance of their traditional duties. These misguided people seek to deprive these people of their rights regarding the temples. Thus these people feel greatly insecure. So this order in the name of His Majesty that after the receipt of this order it should be ensured that no person causes any obstruction to the Brahmins and Hindus of the area so that these people may continue to pray for eternal life for us. Implementation of this order is a must."

Dr. Tara Chand has succinctly summed up this phenomenon with the comment: "As the storm of conquest abated and Hindus and Muslims began to live as neighbours, the long association led to efforts for understanding each other's ideas, habits, nature, rites and rituals. Soon enough there developed harmony between the two."

A major role in this process was played by the Muslim Sufis who had been interacting with the local population with the islamic message of unity and equality. It appealed especially to those sections of society which had been facing discrimination under the existing religious practices marked by the rigid caste system. The Muslim sufis had their counterparts among Hindus, the *sadhus* and *bhaktas*. Dr. Tara Chand recognises the influence of Islam in the growth of Bhakti and reform movements among the Hindus.

The sufis won the hearts of the local people because they showed respect for their customary practices. For example, Sheikh Nizamuddin Auliya, on seeing some Hindus offering prayers in their own way, remarked: *Har qaum raast rahe, deene wa qibla-gake*". (Each community on the true path has its own faith and object of worship).

The Impact of Muslim Rule

The *sulh-e-kul* approach not only made for stability of rule by Muslim kings but also yielded high quality cultural fruits. Interface of civilisations, especially when they are highly developed, invariably results in a new synthesis without obliterating the distinctive features of either. Islam influenced the existing religion, social customs, architecture, painting, literature as also the political thinking of people. So far as religious thought was concerned the dormant and implicit unitarianism of the Vedic and Upanishadic philosophies became more prominent in the *Bhakti* tradition which flourished during this period. On the other hand Muslim Sufis, who proved to be the most successful propagators of Islam, adopted a whole lot of Hindu practices, including the colour of dress. Art and architecture of this period also demonstrates the give and take that had gone on.

A major impact is seen on the language and literature. Sanskrit yielded place to Persian, especially in northern India where the rulers had come from the Persian-speaking regions of central and western Asia. Islam's stress on human equality coupled with the rulers' need to establish rapprochement with common people, brought about a subtle though basic change. The focus shifted from the elite to the common people. Not that it made for people's government or democracy in the modern sense but it brought people at the grassroots into reckoning. Communication with them was not easy through the medium either of Sanskrit or Persian. So while the religious and political elite continued the use of these languages, local folk languages assumed importance and began to be used for literary creations. Literary masterpieces came to be produced in regional languages like Punjabi, Bengali, Gujarati and Marathi and in this development the Sufis and Bhakti saints made significant contribution.

One outstanding product of this commingling was the evolution of a language, Urdu, which captured the heart and mind of the intellectual elite, especially in north India. Over time it contributed richly to the evolution of its Hindi variety with the only difference that the latter derived its literary diction from Sanskrit just as Urdu was basing itself on Persian. Most writers of the period, irrespective of religious affiliation, had a grounding both in Sanskrit and Persian. Just as Hindus took to writing in Persian quite a few Muslim intellectuals studied Sanskrit and used it as a medium of expression. So far as Urdu is concerned it became the favourite of all and thus developed into a kind of lingua franca making cross-country communication possible. It became the vehicle of the common culture that was taking shape as a result of interaction of the two civilisations.

Islam and Composite Nationalism

Apart from other spheres the contribution of Islam to development of political thought is highly significant and of crucial historical importance. Indian Muslims are often accused of separatism as supporters of the two-nation theory. To be fair it must be realised that this was no impact of Islam as is evident from the fact that most Islamic movements, even when fanatically attached to fundamentals of Islam and opposed to any innovation, opposed the theory as well as its corollary the partition of the sub-continent on religious basis. Muslim separatism was the result not of the teachings or spread of Islam, it was the result of certain developments during the British period which the colonial rulers exploited for their own imperialist ends.

The idea of common nationhood was developed and shared by all Indians irrespective of religious affiliation. Eminent Muslim scholars and divines made a significant contribution to the development of this concept even as they actively participated in the struggle against British colonialism. Hindus on the other hand shared the outrage of Muslims when European powers meted out unjust treatment to the Muslim world. Khilafat and non-cooperation movements are outstanding examples of that. So is the consistent Indian support to the Palestine cause.

Maulana Abul Kalam Azad, for example, held the view:

> "Islam has now as great a claim on the soil of India as Hinduism. If Hinduism has been the religion of the people here for several thousands of years, Islam also has been their religion for a thousand years. Just as a Hindu can declare with pride that he is an Indian and follows Hinduism, so also can we say with equal pride that we are Indians and we follow Islam. I shall enlarge this orbit still further. The Indian Christian is equally entitled to say with pride that he is an Indian and he is following a religion of India, namely, Christianity."

In the context of Hindu-Muslim relations he laid the greatest emphasis on harmony between the two, saying that without it all hope of independence, survival and progress of the country would be an idle dream. Without it not only will it be impossible to attain national independence but we shall fail to develop in ourselves the basic attributes and values of humanity. "Therefore even if an angel descends from high heavens and proclaims from the top of Qutub Minar that Swaraj would come within 24 hours if we renounce the goal of Hindu-Muslim unity my response would be to renounce Swaraj but not unity. Because, if Swaraj is delayed, it would be loss only of India but if we lose unity it would be a loss for entire humanity," he declared.

The spearhead of common nationhood and harmony among religions was Mahatma Gandhi. His response to religion-centred nationalism or the so-called 'two nation theory' was: "The 'two nations' theory is an untruth. The vast majority of Muslims of India are converts to Islam or are the descendents of converts. They did not become a separate nation, as soon as they became converts. A Bengali Muslim speaks the same tongue that a Bengali Hindu does, eats the same food and has the same amusements, as his Hindu neighbour. They dress alike. I have often found it difficult to distinguish by outward sign, between a Bengali Hindu and a Bengali Muslim. The same phenomenon is observable more or less in the south among the poor who constitute the masses of India.

> "When I first met the late Sir Ali Imam, I did not know that he was not a Hindu. His speech, his dress, his manners, his food were the same as of the majority of the Hindus in whose midst I found him. His name alone betrayed him. Not even that with Qaid-e-Azam Jinnah. For his name could be that of any Hindu. When I first met him, I did not know that he was a Muslim. I came to know his religion, when I had his full name given to me. His nationality was written in his face and in his

manner. The reader will be surprised to know that for days, if not months, I used to think of the late Vithalbhai Patel as a Muslim, as he used to sport a beard and a Turkish cap. The Hindu law of inheritance governs many Muslim groups. Sir Mahammed Iqbal used to speak with pride of his Brahminical descent. Iqbal and Kitchlew are names common to Hindus and Muslims. Hindus and Muslims of India are not two nations. Those whom God has made one, man will never be able to divide."

That is the best testimony of how harmoniously the two civilisations commingled and interpenetrated. Gandhi's views were endorsed by leading Islamic intellectuals of the time.

In one of his lectures Sir Sayyed thus exhorted his Muslim audience:

"We came into this country even as did the enlightened communities of Hindus. Hindus forgot about the land of their origin and their period of migration and made this country their homeland. They recognised this land between the Himalayas and the Vindhyachal as their homeland. We also left our land centuries ago. We have no memories of those climates, the beauty of those environments, the freshness and taste of those fruits. Nor do we remember the blessings of the holy land of sands and stones. We too adopted this as our homeland and made it our abode. Thus, Hindostan alone is the homeland of both. We breathe the air of Hindostan and eat its food. We are sharers in life and death. Our blood has undergone transformation through intermingling and our complexions and appearances have developed similarity, The Mussalmans have adopted several Hindu customs even as the Hindus have taken to Muslim habits.

So much so that our interaction has created a new language, Urdu, which was neither our language nor theirs.

"So, if we ignore that aspect of our being which is related to God we are one nation as inhabitants of this land. Progress and welfare of the country as well as of both of us, therefore, is possible through unity, mutual sympathy and love. On the other hand disunity and ill-will will destroy both. Woe to those who do not understand this and seek to promote differences between the two communities, for they do not realise that they would themselves be the victims of its disastrous consequences; they inflict injury on themselves."

Maulana Hussain Ahmad Madni similarly stressed the commonness of interests between various communities and wrote:

"Who can deny that whatever difference there be among them on issues of religion they are stringed together as Hindostanis (Indians). This relationship makes their interests common. As Indians whatever is good for a Hindu is good for a Mussalman and what is harmful for the Mussalman is inevitably harmful for the Hindu. Thus their nation and nationhood is the same."

These ideas reflect the authentic Indian response to Islam and of its true followers to India. As a result of this interaction has developed an ethos which we have inherited and which is embodied in our Constitution. There is a common nationhood and a common culture and a never-dying desire to co-operate with all neighbours.

Sufi Tradition and its Impact on Religious Thought

Khwaja Hasan Sani Nizami

Islam and Sufism

The Sufi tradition, in reality, is an Islamic tradition. It only emphasises that mere apparent knowledge of Islam is not sufficient. One should also know the dimensions of *Tauheed*, the concept of 'Unity of God' which was perceived and understood during the lifetime of the Prophet of Islam and has since become remote and distant. "*Tasawwuff*" in my humble view is the way of taking the man, particularly Muslims, out of the "confines"; of the limited world view to the unlimited one.

Let the "unlimited" here not be misunderstood with confusion and anarchy. It may be likened to a never ending scientific exploration or discovery. The discovery is done in a strictly disciplined way. The seeker of God (*Salik*) first travels from the limited to the "Beyond". From then onwards, he goes to the "Infinite".

Man's incapacity in not being able to see *Haq*, Truth, in the "*Khalq* created World, which lies hidden in it, and when he considers the Creation, the "*Khalq*" "*Ghair*" "the other one" from *Haq*, Sufis call it "Farq". They quote Quran, which says:

God is first and the last. The Evident and the Hidden.

In Sufi terminology the opposite of "*Farq*" is "*Jam'a*" that the seeker perceives "Haq", "Truth" without taking note of the "Khalq", the creation, in that way, *Haq* veils *Khalq*, the creation. This is the state of *Fana*. This is also called *Fana Fillah*. To become oblivious of the existence of creation; and to being with God. But this state is not the ultimate object. The next and the higher stage for the seeker is to see the *khalq*, the creation as a manifestation of the attributes of the creator in its variety. This is called *Jama-ul Jama* or *Baqa Billah*. To be with the Creator and to exist with the Creator. There is no state beyond this, as here an object is seen exactly as it is. The seeker finds and sees diversity in unity and unity in diversity in such a way that neither *Haq* veils *Khalq* nor *Khalq* veils *Haq*!

Categories of Sufis

Shaikh Kalimullah Jahanabdi says the excellence lies in a seeker reaching the bounds of *Fana Fillah* and then becoming eternal with the eternity of God.

The first journey (*Fana Fillah*) is called the journey towards God *Sair Fiallah* while the second journey (*Baqa Billah*) is called the journey into God *Sair Fillah*. There is a specified goal of the first journey but there is no end to the other.

Shaiksh Shahabuddin Suharwardy says that apart from the Prophets, there are two categories of those who reached God. The first category is of Mashaikhs and Sufis who reached God by faithfully following the way of Prophet Mohammed (Peace be upon Him) and were deputed for the guidance of mankind. They are also called *Kamil-o-Mukammil*, perfect and able to make others perfect, because they are eternally blessed and graced. They went deep in the sea of *Jam'a-o-Tauheed*, reaching safely on the shore of *Tafreqa* and attaining eternity only after merging into *Fana*. These seekers attained *Baqa*, eternity so that they may perform the task of guidance of mankind.

The other category is of seekers who did not return to this world after attaining communion with God and could not experience the two separate states of *Fana* and *Baqa*. The Prophets have a higher station than that of *Wallis* because even after reaching God they are ever anxious to return towards Creation to guide the human kind.

In the *khilqfat nameh* issued by renowned Sufi Saint Hazrat Shaikh Nizamuddin Aulia to Hazrat Shaikh Shamsuddin Yahya he bases his guidelines on the following *Hadis* or tradition of the Prophet of Islam:

> "If you like I can swear by God in whose hands is my life that those humans are nearest to God who love humanity for the sake of God, and love God through mankind."

The essence of this teaching was, that no seeker could reach the highest spiritual stage unless he keeps good company with creatures of God. The Prophet (PBUH) also gave strict orders to Muslims to be good with their neighbours. He even said that it is not sufficient that your neighbours are not unhappy with you; they should be happy with you. He also defined the neighbourhood as up to forty houses on every side of your own house.

Coming of Sufis to India

The first organised Sufi migration to India was through Hazrat Shaikh Moinuddin and his Mureeds of Chishti Sufi Order or *Silsilah*. In observing faithfully the teachings of the Prophet of Islam (PBUH) they gave utmost importance to the Indian people with whom they had to live. Sufi Hamiduddin was one of the Khalifas or preachers of Hazrat Khwaja Ajmeri. He was stationed at Nagaur Rajasthan. In Nagaur majority of the local inhabitants were vegetarian. Sufi Hameeduddin after reaching Nagaur made it obligatory for people coming to see him that they should not bring non-vegetarian food with them as it can hurt the feelings of the local people. That tradition is still maintained in his eight century old *Khanqah*. In the *Dargah* of Hazrat Khwaja Moinuddin Chishti even onion and garlic were never used in the official *Langar* (public kitchen) utensils; as many Indian sects dislike them like they dislike meat. This is very interesting to note that the Prophet of Islam himself advised his followers, not to use raw onions and garlic while visiting mosques! Perhaps for their smell!

Hazrat Khwaja Ajmeri's Khalifa in the third generation, Hazrat Baba Farid started teaching *Zikr* or recitation of the name of Allah in local Punjabi-Saraiki language. These things removed all kinds of barriers between the newcomers and the local people. It even opened the gates for exchange of religious knowledge and ideas between them. Hazrat Khwaja Nizamuddin Aulia the well known scholar and Sufi Saint narrates the visit of a lone Hindu *Jogi* in the *Khanqah* of his Master Hazrat Baba Farid, thus:

> It appears that the *Jogi* was certainly a welcome visitor. He went to the *Khanqah* without any

hesitation. It was the period of Khwaja Nizamuddin Aulia's spiritual training in the *Khanqah*. Khwaja asked the *jogi*, "which way you go? What is your discipline? What is the basis of your teaching and practice?" The jogi replied, "We were taught that there are two parts of a human being. One is the higher one and the other lower. The higher station in the body is from head to the navel, and the lower is from navel to feet. The good result comes out thus when we observe truthfulness, sincerity, purity, morals and good conduct by the higher portion of the body. And watch the lower part with purity, chastity and good permitted actions."

Sufis and Yogis

The Khwaja much admired the sayings of the *jogi*. Interactions with people like the above may appear uncommon; however, they are numerous. Both sides accepted what was thought beneficial and rejected the rest. In the *Malfuzat* of Hazrat Khwaja Nizamuddin Aulia another incident is mentioned when a *jogi* came to the Khanqah and said that nowadays children are born with infected dispositions because we do not know the proper and auspicious time to go to our spouses.

The Khwaja took paper and pen to note down the proper times for that matrimonial duty. But his master Baba Farid intervened and said, please do not write these things. There is no benefit for you in it.

In another episode one *jogi* tried to present an aphrodisiac to Hazrat Gesudaraz Banda Nawaz on the assumption that Muslims are allowed four wives. And the poor *jogi* because of his *brahamcharya* was tired of celibacy, the medicine was lying without any use. But the Khwaja was very angry on the offer made and the jogi later apologised. From then on, I think he became aware that Islam is not a religion of four wives alone.

We see a new phenomenon in the early sufi history of India. Although most of the sufis were followers of the Hanafi school of Muslim Jurisprudence some of them, particularly Hazrat Khwaj'a Nizamuddin Aulia took the liberty to refer directly to Qur'an and tradition of the Prophet instead of reaching there through Imam Abu Hanifa. For example when Sultan Ghiasuddin Tughlaq called the Shaikh to a gathering of Ulama to prove the permissibility of the practice of listening to *sam'a*, the sufi music which was not allowed in Islam according to the opinion of the Ulama the Shaikh, instead of quoting the opinion of Iman Abu Hanifa quoted a *Hadis*. After coming back from the gathering of Ulama the Shaikh asked one of his learned Mureeds, Maulana Fakhruddin Zarradi to write down the arguments in favour of permissibility of *sam'a*. The Maulana obeyed, and in the very first paragraph of his write-up gave the historical definition of a Sufi in these words:

> *A Sufi' is a person who does not restrict himself to any one and particular school of Islamic Jurisprudence!*

That statement was a revolutionary statement and influenced not only Muslims but followers of other faiths also. Many reformist movements started after that and Kabir and many other saints took inspiration from it and struggled hard to broad base the Indian religious thought. The most successful effort in this direction is the Sikh religion in which the revered Guru very large heartedly presented the essence of many religions in one fine unit including the teachings of the famous and representative Sufi Saint, Hazrat Shaikh Farid Ganje-e-Shakar.

The Muslims came to India in many guises. There were invaders with their armies and orthodox'Ulama, the traditional scholars of the faith. There were traders and also there were Sufis, who shunned the kings and their courts. In India almost every thing was new for them. The kings and the ruling class had to deal with their subjects but till the Mughal period they tried to keep a safe distance between themselves and the ruled population like the British for political and administrative reasons. The'Ulama, orthodox Muslim scholars were more cautious. From the very beginning to the end they tried their best to keep themselves and their followers away not only from the local Indian beliefs but also from Indian customs in order to safeguard and protect their own beliefs and customs. The Sufis as true Muslims were also enthusiastic about their Islamic beliefs and behaviour but they were also aware of the concept of the unity of Creator and His creation. They knew the "system" and "discipline" to obey and show their love to the Creator and how to please the Creator by pleasing and serving his creation, particularly mankind.

They were also aware of the fact that Islam never claimed to be a new religion. The Prophet always said that many other prophets and guides from God came before him. As their teachings were changed and distorted so after sometime the need was felt for a new guide, who could show the right direction and the true path. In short, the attitude of Sufis was rather liberal. The Sufi history of India shows that they always bypassed the conflict and strove to the points of agreement. As far as Islamic Jurisprudence, the *Fiqh*, is concerned, majority of Muslims follow particular schools of *Fiqh* like Jafari, Maliki Hambali, Hanafi. Shafi'l etc. But sometimes Sufis, inspite of the fact that they are *muqallids* and followers of a particular Imam of *fiqh*, they directly refer to the original source of Qur'an and *hadis*, the tradition of the Prophet for deriving the rules and regulations needed for local requirements. For example the Sufi order of the patron saint of India, Hazrat Khwaja Moinuddin Chishti Ajmeri, allowed Sufi music *sam 'a* and his khalifa or representative in the third generation of the order, Hazrat Khwaja Nizamuddin Aulia took advantage of that liberalism because music was considered not only helpful for seekers of God generally but was thought to be an essential part of the Indian psyche.

Muslims and Pre-Islamic Customs

A new situation appeared in those days when local people embraced Islam in large numbers. They were very particular in observing semi-religious customs and rituals. It was not easy for them to leave those traditions which had become part of their life. For example they used to wear a cotton thread, the *Janeo*, used to light lamps for the well being of their children in temples and they were very fond of going to *Tirth Yatras.* The company of orthodox' Ulama was very frightening for them as ail these habits of new converts were completely unacceptable to the scholars. But for them the help came from Sufi quarters. The size of *Janeo* was shortened, it was given two colours and named *qalawa* or *kalawa*, a symbol of obedience to God as well as to ward off the evil. The symbolic thread itself was converted or thought to be converted to Islam. Likewise, the lightening of lamps was not banned, only the place changed—instead of a temple to a mosque!

The new converts neither knew the basic teachings of their old religion nor were fully aware of the intricacies of the new one. But slowly and gradually they became true Muslims while adding Indian colour to their beliefs and practices. That was the natural result of living and dying together peacefully. One such example is from Panipat, a small town near Delhi. About two centuries back one Muslim scholar had to settle in a purely Hindu inhabited *mohalla*. The wife of the Maulvi Sahib suddenly died during the child birth leaving behind a healthy male baby. Maulvi Sahib was much worried about his new born son because he had no means to arrange a step-mother for him or to move out of the locality. But the help came promptly from the neighbourhood where a Brahmin lady previously had given birth to a female baby. The noble lady offered to feed and look after two babies instead of only one. Thus the famous Sufi saint Hazrat Ghaus Ali Shah Qalandar Panipati was fed and brought up in the house of a Hindu Pandit. Panditji had no male offspring and as the Hindu custom goes, at the time of his and his wife's death all the funeral rites were performed by Hazrat Ghaus Ali Qalandar including the recitation of the *Gyatri Mantr* at Haridwar. I am sure no Muslim mufti or Hindu priest will consider proper what was done by those Brahmin and Maulvi families but that was made easy by the Sufi tradition!

Two Textual Paradigms of Nationalism in the Middle Period Thought of Maulana Azad

Barun De

In the last year, I had been thinking about Maulana Azad as a politician and human being, distinct from the iconic figure into which the Indian national movement sought to transform him. I regret my exiguous knowledge of Hindustani, let alone Urdu; I do not know Persian or Arabic; all familiar languages for the Maulana Saheb. But I am proud to be someone whose grandfather, Brajendranath De, 19th century ICS, the second BA and first MA of Awadh, of Canning College, Lucknow, who edited and translated the *Tabaqat-i-Akbari* of Bakshi Nizamuddin Ahmad, established a heritage for me at least in which Hinduism and Islam were not completely distinct; and gave pride in my ancestral faith in the Brahmo Samaj's Upanishadic creed, with due weight to the monotheism of Islam and the simple piety of the Guru Granth Sahib as superior to what Brahmos dislike as the rank polytheism of popular Hinduism.

I speak with respect of India's Maulana, without the privilege of reading him in the original and write about him as an Indian, whose works have been translated by Indians into

English. I hoped when I was first invited to present this paper to write about the interaction between British colonialism and India as reflected in his writings. But reading the translations and summary of some of the originals, Syeda Saiyidain Hameed, edited in *India's Maulana: Abul Kalam Azad*, I found less about imperialism and more about internal problems faced in the first half of the 20th century, as he saw them. What there was about colonialism, were flat statements about its predatory and destructive weight on Indian life, and particularly on Islam, crushed and humiliated, as the Maulana saw it, in the 19th century; about Islam and Hinduism seeking to transcend its segmentation and divisiveness.[1] There was far more on the positive side about how one could transcend these negative aspects, a synthesis of what the Maulana in late 1927, in a series of articles in the second series of *al-Hilal* (proscribed by the British in 1915), *i.e. al-Hilal 'sani'* edited by his disciple Abdur Razzaq Malihabadi, called, Nationalism.[2] It is necessary to go more into the Maulana's own understanding of what nationalism was.

Three Phases of Azad's Thoughts

For the present, I take up the middle of his thought. Azad's serial and political thought can be divided into three phases. The first period is very well known and recently written about during the observance of the Azad Centenary in India, by the editors of the biography by Ian Henderson Douglas, and by V.N. Datta.[3] The second is from the time of the Maulana joining the Khilafat movement led by Mahatma Gandhi — even more than its Muslim aspect led by the Ali

Brothers and Maulana Abdul Bari of Firangi Mahal, Lucknow—till his presidential speech at the Ramgarh Indian National Congress at 1940. The third is his eclipse by the forces of majoritarian Indian nationalism and Pakistani communalism, as the Second World War rose to a crescendo and then after it in the tragic partition of India and his transformation by the Indian state into a cultural-spiritual icon.

Azad, earlier a militant revolutionary realised after the First World War and his release from internment in Ranchi by his British jailors, that the best way for India's path to independence was by joining Gandhi's movement for Hind Swaraj, Satyagraha and Ahimsa, instead of quixotic *jehad* by mujahidin across the North-West Frontier[6] all the way from Kabul to Meshed and Tashkent'. In fact, even earlier in Ranchi, his ruminations about his Islamic genealogy back to the days of Ahmad Shah Abdali, the Mughals and the Delhi Sultans, as copied by his adviser, Fazliddin in the *Tazkira*, shows his becoming aware of the need to move from revolutionary militancy towards non-responsive detachment from the policies and practices of a repressive state. The identity-crisis which Azad had been going through since he gave up his claims to his father and elder brother's *pirship* to start his own journalistic *jehadi* seminary through *al-Hilal* and *al-Balagh* was over when the Maulana came back to Indian civil society, not by forsaking Pan-Islam, but by wedding it to Gandhian espousal of the good and the true by means of non-violence, seeking to give the Khilafat movement and later Indian Islam, a clearly Indian ideology — as indeed other Indian Muslim leaders like Hakim Ajmal Khan or Dr. Ansari were also doing in this period. All this has been described by many scholars and most recently in V.N. Datta's sober and cadenced praise. But a close look at two texts of his ideas about nationalism as they evolved in his middle-period will still be worthwhile.

The Congress Presidential Speech at the Delhi Special Session, 1923

The shift from Islamic reformisms to syncretic Indian nationalism is clearly previsaged in Azad's first Congress Presidential speech. This was after the Khilafat agitation had met with imperialistic repression and imprisonment, and Gandhi had withdrawn his Satyagraha, after the Chauri Chaura violence. Out of custody, Congress leaders were in contradiction about social reform or political utilisation of British Indian legislation — the no-changers and the pro-changers. Also cracking Congress' integrity were the growing riotousness of Hindu and counter dependent Muslim revivalist movements, *Tanzim* and *Tabligh* (spawned by the Khilafat movement's fanatical figures) and of *Shuddhi* and *Sangathan* sparked off by Arya Samaji pietism. A special session of the Congress was convened at Delhi in 1923 after Gandhi's Bardoli Resolution lifting the Non- Cooperation movement. Certain passages in the speech bear recall seventy-five years after, for their contemporary relevance to India's heritage of internationalist fraternity with the Afro-Asian Islamic world, as well as its subcontinental tensions within, on questions of confessional faith.[4]

Speaking in retrospect — in the contest of the Khilafat movement of the fall and rise of Turkey after the First World War, Azad said:

> Ghazi Mustafa Kamal Pasha's hands have not

> only shaken up the sleeping destiny of Turkey, they have knocked at all the doors in the East.
>
> ...In fact, India commends the spirit of every Eastern nation which is fighting for freedom, and feels chagrin for every nation which is lagging behind in these endeavours. India assures the patriots of Egypt, Syria, Palestine, Iraq, Morocco and other Eastern countries that ... their freedom is no less dear to us than our own Independence... Due to the Khilafat movement, the Hindu-Muslim issue, without which India's freedom would be a shattered dream, was resolved, and the obstacles which were blocking its progress for a long time, were overcome.

Going on to elaborate on what he called 'our superstructure' of Congress nationalist ideology of non-violence, and the new controversy between Swarajists and no-changers, he however premised new problems of' 'the foundation', *i.e.* Hindu-Muslim unity...'Without this foundation, our freedom and all the factors of our country's life and progress will remain a dream. Without it, once again, we cannot create, within ourselves, the primary principles of humanism.' And then came his article of secular faith, one of his most famous sentences:

> Today if an angel were to descend from the heaven and declare from the top of the Qutub Minar, that India will get Swaraj within twenty four hours provided she relinquishes Hindu-Muslim unity, I will relinquish Swaraj rather than give up Hindu-Muslim unity. Delay in the attainment of Swaraj will be a loss to India, but if our unity is lost it will be a loss

for entire mankind.

These words acquired poignance in the context of colonialist partition of India in August 1947, the consequences of which still bedevil South Asia more than fifty years after the event, in the shape of fratricidal alarms and excursions, which spill over across borders.

What is of equal poignance for India today are Azad's explication why fresh obstacles had developed in the resolution of the problems of social unity based on concordance of faiths in support for leaders of a structure of political Islam, which was imperilled by the common enemy of both Hindus and Muslims, Western colonialism.

> "Four years ago, we made a grand announcement to the world, filled with national pride we asked the world to stand by and wait for our freedom. But the moment the world's attention was focused on us, a different story became evident of our shamelessness and bloodshed...'Save the Hindus from Muslims' says one group.'Save Islam from Hinduism' says another. When the order of the day is 'Protect Hindus' and 'Protect Muslims' who cares about protecting the nation? The press and platform are busy fanning bigotry and obscurantism, while a duped and ignorant public is busy shedding blood on the streets. Bloody riots have occurred at Ajmer, Palwal, Saharanpur, Agra and Meerut. Who can say where these unfortunate consequences will lead?"

This analysis gains more depth in the next lines which bespeak communalist provocation by minorities in the rhetoric of national causes, and far more violent right-wing majoritarian backlash of counter-communalism seeking strength in numbers.

> 'It was not so long ago that the Muslims, as a community took no part in the activities of the Congress. They felt that being small in number, and deprived of wealth and education they could not afford to participate in any national struggle... 'they confined themselves to communal organisations. Those of you who have been studying changes in Muslim corporate life during the last twelve years know that mine was the first voice raised in 1912 against this attitude. I said..' my Muslim brethren' should trust their Hindu brothers, abandon the policy of communalism, join Congress and make the country's freedom their ultimate goal. At that time my message was not well received by my Muslim brethren. I found strong opposition to my views. But not long after that the Muslims recognised the truth. In 1916 when I was interned at Ranchi, I heard that a large number of Muslims were entering the fold of Congress'.

Azad refers here to the 1916 beginnings of accord between Muslim politicians and the predominantly Hindu politicians in the Congress (with the exception of a few in Western India like Muhammad Ali Jinnah) at Lucknow and subsequent meeting of the All-India Muslim League also at Lucknow. As was to be his wont in later years, when he became isolated from Muslim communalism he raised his voice in pride in challenging that trend. This came out of shared agitation against arbitrary colonial actions in North India as well as out of Muslim mass resentment about the beginning of

European dismemberment of the carcass of the 'sick man of Europe', the Ottoman Empire, beginning from Italy's Tripoli War of 1912-13.

He continues:

> Just as: I raised my voice against the Muslims and fear of their opposition did not deter me from the truth, so also today, I consider it my sacred duty to raise my voice against my brothers who are hosting the flag of Hindu *Sangathan.* I am surprised to see that the mentality of the Muslim political circles of those days is being mirrored among these people today. But whereas the Muslims were prompted by the fear of their numerical inferiority, these excitable people are four times the number of Muslims. I declare, without hesitation, that India wants neither a Hindu nor Muslim *Sangathan.* We require one single *Sangathan*—the Indian National Congress.
>
> Some responsible leaders of the *Shuddhi* movement assert that it is not opposed to Hindu-Muslim unity. Therefore, after preaching opposition, they end on a note of cordiality and love. To these gentlemen, I would suggest that having already led us along the wrong path... do you believe that having excited the passions of jealousy and revenge, you can continue the business of cordiality and love.
>
> While, in theory, we can separate our common struggle for political salvation, in practice we cannot keep them in different compartments. We want composite nationhood. It will, however, be impossible

to create an atmosphere of harmony when slogans of *Malech* (sic.)[5] are being raised at one quarter, while the other is resounding with cries of *Kafir.*

Azad's Presidential Address

The explication of this counter dependence of communalist politics stands out starkly in Azad's Presidential Speech to the 1923 Congress. Students of Indian politics today are well aware of the way in which, since the mid-1980s the previously more secularist Congress party was swung by reactionary vote bank considerations against the cause of a common civil code and gender justice, following the Shah Bano case judgment in the Supreme Court, the way Sikh fundamentalism of the Dam Dami Taksal variety was allowed to permeate fundamentalist consciousness in the Punjab in the vain attempt of a Congress authoritarian managerial segment to combat Akali Sikh communal opposition to the Congress, the way in which communal organisations networking and propaganda led to neo-Hindu backlash led by the Bharatiya Janata Party as head of 'the Sangh Parivar'. On the crest of this Congress' representation of Indian nationality was contested and challenged — a representation Azad had supported since his release from British internment in 1918.

Not 'one Sangathan' alone as Azad believed in 1923, but secularist plurality and diversity, loosening and lubricating the variety of levers of South Asian democracy were then, and still are, necessary to energise as a harmonious whole; not just the Hindu-Muslim unity that the Maulana desired, but the entire variety of religious, linguistic and caste friction in 'a mirror crack'd from side to side' that British India and its Dependencies, or even vivisected Independent India reflects. Only an inkling of this is to be found in the Maulana's adjective of 'composite' for 'nationhood'.

How would this compositeness develop in his view? He has a cryptic and peremptory sentence in 1923:

> Let me remind you that we should without further delay prepare a national pact which will not only define our goal, but will also give a verdict on the daily clashes and future relationships of all the communities that make up our country.[7]

Elements of such an agenda of what today would be called 'Intra-Communal Accord' did occupy the politicians of British India in the rest of the quotidian struggle till 1935 through Swarajist 'Council Entry', the Sirajganj 'Pact', between Hindu and Muslim politicians in Bengal's elective bodies briefly engineered by Deshbandhu Chittaranjan Das till his untimely death in Darjeeling in 1925, renewed communal riots, the Motilal Nehru Report, the prelude to which was one of the last serious attempts at mutual accommodation to eschew majoritarianism among Indian leaders from Jinnah and Sapru through Ansari and Azad to Motilal. All efforts, however, were negated by the dominance of British style constitutionalist reservations policy which Muslim communalism espoused in the 1930s and which had been explicated even earlier than 1935 by the Morley-Minto reforms; the all-white Simon Commission's Report, the Communal Award and finally the Government of India Act of 1935. Suffice it here to say that Azad stood on the same side as Chittaranjan Das' Pact of 1925 as well as the anti-communalism of the Nehrus. But like them he failed to present any radical alternative to the increasing decolonising policies of'Divide and Rule' in the Indus basin (later West

Pakistan) or the Ganga-Brahmaputra-Meghna lower delta (out of which East Pakistan was later carved).

The 1923 Congress Presidential Address is only one paradigm of a liberal Muslim nationalist's approach to composite Indian nationality. Explicitly Muslim and implicitly Pan-islamic in its tenor and sympathies (witness his stress on the freedom struggle in West Asia, but not in China where nationalism and incipient socialism were locked in conflict with warlordism backed by colonialism, Japanese as well as Western): witness also his critique of *Shuddhi* and *Sangathan* and relative silence about the forces of *Tabligh* and *Tanzim* which were raising their voices in the vacuum created by the defeat of the Khilafat/ Sultanate of Turkey (defeated by the West European powers after the War, but destroyed by Ghazi Mustafa Kamal Pasha and his new secularist government).[8]

This tenor is one of natural biases and not of any failure of relative objectivity. Azad obviously felt that the raising of Hindu communal slogans in the dogdays after the collapse of Khilafat and the outbreaks of mob violence in 1922-23 were greater dangers to India's national movement than minority sentiments which a healthy national struggle could take in its stride.

From the time he edited '*al-Hilal*' (The Crescent) 1912-14 and '*al-Balagh*' (The Trumpet—brought out, when the British suppressed *al-Hilal* in 1914, and itself, suppressed in 1915) Azad sought to arouse anti-colonialist sentiment on the basis of patriotism, and patriotism alone, leavened by faith in the Quranic tenets and firm love for kin and fatherland. He believed that this alone could bring his people out of subjection. He had himself not clarified in the *al-Hilal* articles the distinction between 'people' and 'nation' occulted by the word '*qaum*', which can mean any community between sept or tribe to sect or linguistic subgroup. This occlusion that led even him more *avant-garde* in this respect, than many contemporary Sikh, Jain, Christian (or Anglo-Indian), Hindu or Muslim leaders of opinion to see the need for a 'national pact' i.e. of 'federation' so to speak between religious communities, and to emphasise only the two major numerical communities. Significantly he was silent about the problems of Sikhs *vis-a-vis* resurgent Hinduism of the Arya Samaj variety in a Punjab which then stretched from Attock to the environs of Delhi and to Sialkot, as well as Ambala in Haryana and Shimla in Himachal Pradesh (none of which states then existed). These problems had already given rise to the Akali movement for Gurdwara cleansing of princely or Hindu *mahant* influence, with which Congress had sympathised within the Non-Cooperation Movement phase. He was not aware of Christian Nagas and Mites in the far north-eastern borders next to Burma, or for that matter, of Indians in Burma, then—till 1935—a part of British India. *Avant garde* Azad certainly was both—as Muslim and nationalist. But he could hardly have thought ahead of his times when community and nationality had not been disentangled in elite nationalism.

It is certainly not appropriate for a generation of young historians in the late 20th century to ignore him as a Nehruvian statist, while they wink at nationality being narrowly equated once again in South Asia with ethnic community, whether in the fringes of the vale of Kashmir or in North-East India or in the majoritarianism of Bangladeshi peasant permeation among the tribal people of the Chittagong Hill Tracts—or, to take a non-South-Asian view; among the Myammarese who seek to dominate the tribal or cultivating minority peoples, Rakhaingis, Kachin, Shan or Karenni of old Burma; or, the *madrasa* trained Taliban Afghan refugees sheltered by Pakistan and now courted by Turkmenistan (who seek to subjugate to fundamentalism the Turkomen, Hazaras, Uzbegs, Tajiks or Nuristanis of Northern Afghanistan across the Hindu Kush as it slopes to the Amu Darya).

It will be worth studying Azad's pilgrim's progress through the conceptual hurdles of federating minority politics.

Islam and Nationalism 1927

Four years after the 1923 speech, Azad clarified his position at the time of the Nehru Report. An article prepared for a fresh version of 'al-Hilal' (known as 'al-Hilal Sani' or Crescent the Second) from June-December, 1927, edited by his journalistic successor, Abdur Razzaq Malihabadi, has been translated by Dr. S.S. Hameed in her edition of *India's Maulana*, Vol. II. In it, he goes beyond the then dead issue of Khilafat and confronts those who had read his 1912-14 consonance with the 'narrow mindedness of patriotism', as well as those who felt that pan-Islam among Indian Muslims was not compatible with 'interest in the political problems of their own country'.[9] The purpose of this article, he said was 'to search for a middle course of a multi-dimensional problem'. He then proceeded to give an Islamic definition of a European term, a definition which he believed was universalistic in the spirit of the Prophet Muhammad's statement in each of the five daily prayers' affirming Allah, affirming also his slave and messenger the Prophet that 'God, our Lord and the Lord of our Universe, I confess that all your people are brothers, and whatever differences they may have created among themselves, you have created them as one human race.' The Maulana proceeded to move from Islamic 'people' to give a encompassing definition.

> What is Nationalism? It is the concept for a special state of man's collective consciousness and a nation of social order. It distinguishes one group of people from another and makes it possible for a large number of them to come together to lead their lives and undertake their collective responsibilities.'[10]

This was a permissive definition, inclusive of many forms of social relations in ordered formation. It has neither 'race, country, colour or language' exclusivity—'four great obstacles in the way of universal human brotherhood' and that Azad specifically reprobated in his praise of the Muslim daily prayer nor the specificities which the modern connotation of nationalism demand—of statehood, citizenship, nationality and subjugation to particular territorial laws. In this sense, Azad continued the 'first *al-Hilal*' connotation of unity and universalism of humanity, whose core to him was Quranic precept. This definition was closer to Pan-Islam than to Anglican territoriality—Azad reprobates Cicero's 'Roman', not humanist, nationalism. By association thus, he accepts neither modern Christian nor European nationalism, but rather Islam. The argument runs a twisted course. It makes connectivity and concordance the hallmark of current social order. It proceeds to posit that mankind starts with simple, and proceeds to complex affinities—first to temporary and then permanent abode, then from 'city-state' to patriotism and then to the 'nationalist' unification of different tribes. Azad then races ahead logically into wider orbits of unification, till unity of all is reached:

> The chain of relative extensions ends with the

> continental division. The final stage where this process of evolution reaches maturity and completion is the stage of 'Humanism' and 'Universalism'. At this stage man realises that the boundaries and relative affiliations of human association and areas that he had created were not actual and neutral. True relationship is only one, the entire earth is man's native land, mankind one family, and all human beings are brothers... the only and perfect unity the unity of the human race, created by God Almighty, manifests itself.[11]

This was an idealist view, which may not appear at all familiar to modern social science analysts of nationalism. Nevertheless many Asians and Africans as well as Europeans in the Tsarist-Soviet domains related to it in the early twentieth century, when nation-states as distinct from subject peoples were becoming common in Asia and Africa. It certainly fitted with the amorphous condition of the peoples of South Asia in the era of the emergence of the Congress to dominance in all India politics.

In the 1920s, Islam and Hinduism emerged as competing claimants for group identity. Azad's approach was utilitarian—of seeking to bring the widest number of people within a consensus by catering to the widest possible definition of the public good and by 'trimming' sails, ideologically, to cross-current winds. In 1927, lacking the focus of a Pan-Islamist issue such as Khilafat, Azad, one of the most advanced Muslim modernists of the time in Asia, was hard put to it to define Islamic nationalism *per se*.

He did this by the device of 'territoriality'.

For mankind, scattered all over the world, it was necessary to divide themselves into different areas and groups'.[12]

But again, Azad still continued to elaborate on the oecumenical aspect of mediaeval Islam: that too without reference to the discrete civilisations of the Islamic *umma.* Only at the end of this discourse does he face the real problem:

> Islam, therefore, discourages the emergence of narrow orbits. Nationalism, in its simplest form, has existed for ages. But the collective beliefs and ideas that the term brings to mind are the product of the new era of European civilisation. It started as a defence for human rights and liberty, but has, today, become its greatest threat.[13]

These last two pages of the essay as translated by Dr. Saiyidain Hameed show a percipient explication of 'actually-existing' nationalism in the 20th century European-dominated world, Absolutism gave way to popular sovereignty over the nation, but still'confined to Europe and to Europeans'. According to old Roman tenets 'the world was divided into superior and inferior nations' Europe and America determined liberty and rights. Thus:

> At the time when France was preparing herself for the third freedom revolution, no Frenchman felt that Ameer Abdul Qadir Jazairi and his unfortunate people who were subjugated by France through its military might also need freedom. Today the world knows what is being done in Syria by France who claims to be the preacher of 'freedom' and 'nationalism'.[14]

Because of these dual standards of nationalism (what I have elsewhere and earlier called 'two ways of nationalism')[15] there occurred 'an inevitable reaction. Before the 19th century had made much headway, its signs became visible. The lower echelons of society began to realise that, despite talk, real liberty and equality are non-existent.'[16]

The organisation of nations became itself a hindrance to nationalism. Capitalism accentuated the problem. Communism sought to revolutionise society's very structure. Disgusted by nationalist excesses in the first World War, European thinkers and philosophers called for 'unfettered human brotherhood' and 'reorganisation of the world social order'. The world appeared to be moving towards a broader sphere than the present circle within which it is confined.[17]

It appeared in 1927 to the Maulana consequently that in order to establish peace and reform nationalism not only in the Islamic community, but the entire world today may have to act according to the point of view stated in Islam.[18]

This ending brings us back full circle to pan-Islamist universalism. It is obvious that Azad's path had not diverged from *al-Hrilal-awwal* to *al-Hilal sani.* Nationalism was oppressive European state power in actuality, but also bore the possibility of global transcendence as an ideal. He was, like Gandhi, not enamoured of either Capitalism or Communism. But realistically he saw 'the lower echelons of society'—a better term than the current post-Marxist neologism so much favoured by Western socioiogues, i.e.'subaltern'—as dissatisfied with contemporaneous nationality. His instincts led him towards globalising trends, for which Islam was, to him, a sufficient vehicle.

The 'National Pact' Azad had called for in his 1923 oration

receded from his mind, as the country moved towards Congress' Civil Disobedience Movement in the 1930s. But in this article he had clarified the distinction between first way nationalism, which was aggressive and a second way of nationalism, which he believed, could be more humanitarian. The Indian national vision of the Ramgarh Congress Presidential Address of March 1940 still lay in the future.

Towards Ramgarh, 1927-40

The three remaining years of the decade of the 1920s saw Azad torn between politics and religion in new attempts to build Islamic nationalism as a viable component in the Indian national movement. On the one hand, he endeavoured to establish as alternatives to the Muslim League's sectarian landlord-gentry communalism the Indian National Union '1926' and the All-india Nationalist Muslim Party '1929' but none of the two could compete. He sought to trim between League and Congress in getting the Nehru Report accepted unanimously. This failed, marking M.A. Jinnah's London retirement from which the latter emerged in the mid-1930s bent on 'sole spokesman'—ship of the Muslims of British India; while Azad spent two further terms imprisoned as a loyal Congressman in the two Civil Disobedience Movements of 1930-32.

On the other hand, Azad came out by the end of 1927 (after *al-Hilal Sani* closed down) to the stirring of a new intellectual life within the Congress (which, unlike Jinnah, he had not forsaken). Six years after British intelligence officials had pulped his laboriously written drafts of the *Tarjuman-i-Quran*, his prolegomena, to a new interpretation of the innate message of the Quran, thus reducing him to temporary emotional paralysis.

Slowly his pen started moving, on paper. And then the flow was unstoppable if he wanted to stop, he could not, and in a little over two years he had re-written the entire work'.[19]

The *Tarjuman-al-Quran*, the greatest of Azad's texts, marks the fulfillment of his project to make Islam compatible with the circumstances of the land of his ansectors and his heritage. There have been many analyses of the universalism of the *Tarjuman* and its stress on the inner meaning of the *Sura-al-Fatiha*, the first verses of the Quran and on *Rahmat* and *Rububiyat* (benevolence and provision of nourishment) of Allah, the Beneficent, the Merciful, Lord of the Worlds, Owner of the Day of Judgement, whom Muslims implore, calling out '*Ihdenas Siratal Mustaquim Siratal Ladhina an anzta Alayhim*' (show us the Straight Path, the path of those whom thou hast favoured). Azad's interpretation is notable for its stress on benevolence, mercy and righteousness and on the Quranic precept of *lakum dinukum wa liyadin* (to you your way, to me mine). Here he brings together the philosophical concordance of what he believes was Islam's straight path, Christian doctrines of forgiveness, and the multiplicity as well as monotheism in the worship, whether of images or of formless spirit in Hindu practices, plebeian as well as elite. In the realm of philosophy, Azad had accomplished this by 1930. If in the 1908-11 period, he had gone through a crisis of religious identity in the 1920s, he had gone through a crisis of cultural identity. But it required eight to ten more years to explicate this in a political concordance of unity in diversity. Then in the agony of the rest of his life, he would see communalism triumph over his vision of minorities' dignity in diversity, a non-majoritarian democracy, over his own idea of national concordance in a truly national India over the reason of his Ramgarh presidential address of March 1940.

In the next paper on this subject, I propose to deal with Azad as the Congress president during the Second War years and finally as India's Minister for Education and Scientific Research in the context of the changing paradigms of his continuing crisis of identity, which the new shape of partitioned Indian nationality did not permit him to transcend till he died broken-hearted.

Comment on Penultimate Section

I would prefer to take off on a broader tack by elaborating on some points on a text of Maulana Azad on which I spoke yesterday, his 1927 article on '*Islam aur Nationalism*' as a prelude to the thematic of variety of civilisation in Islam.

It is interesting that the Maulana tackled nationalism by categorising nationalism as one among many developmental stages in Islam. The way he put it, it could happen in any religion. I am not now arguing that nationalism is a dependent variable of religion, but only that to the Maulana at a particular time, nationalism was a part of the essential unity of religiosity under Godhead, not necessarily revealed by scriptures (though he certainly believed in the Qur'an as scripture), but through any sound, ethical way of life. His proposition was that mankind starts individually, then humanity organises itself in groups, tribes develops particular ethics, organisation then comes to broader elements than tribes. So ultimately, it moves naturally to that grouping called nationalism. And then, he comes to its actually existing forms.

I am here using the adjectival form'actually existing' in the way it was used in the 1908s and early 1980s for communism. The usage 'actually existing Socialism' as distinct from 'doctrinal Socialism' may be recalled. Azad says, and I think he is correct, varieties of'actually existing' nationalism come up, first in Europe at a certain phase of its history, in the aggressive and militant please of capitalism in the 16th to 20th centuries. He does not use the term 'bourgeoisie', but he does describe colonialism as the externally aggressive aspect of this European capitalism.

Colonialism, Azad proceeds, destroys the life of the emotions, of sentiments, of ethnicity, of the social and moral forces that come under its impact. He focuses on Islamic countries, where the overrule of colonialism was, according to him, always evil or at least harmful. He then proceeds to argue that when nationalism comes as an inevitable stage in countries overruled by colonialism, it proceeds by excluding nationalism. In a series of articles written since 1974, before I had even read Azad's work, and certainly before the spate of Western and subaltern Westernised writings on nationalism, I have referred to'two ways of nationalism' in the same way as Marxists at one time used to carry on a discourse of'two ways of capitalism' — the English or more evolutionary and the Prussian or Junker way: one was gradualist, the other was forced march capitalism.

First way nationalism, in its aggressive, colonialist aspect, systematically destroyed previous webs of life in the territory it conquered. Second way nationalism of the anti-colonial variety had many elements for revitalising or transforming the old webs of society and culture. I emphasise diversity here, more than unity. But the Maulana true to the universalism of the age of Tagore, Gandhi, Iqbal or Nehru, focussed on universality. In 1927, he already noted that people in various parts of the world were talking of universal brotherhood. This was a clear decade before Wendell Wilkie wrote his tract called *One World.* Azad said people were talking of Communism but Islam would surely come to terms with even this according to territorial circumstances. This is a previsaging of later events in his worldview.

We come now to the essentiality for religion as much of nationalism as of territoriality. Territoriality, religion and nationalism are like intersecting circles that we must take pains to distinguish as well as interrelate. Asghar Ali has also emphasised the need for justice as a constituent element in the state form which practises nationalism. This quest for social justice would of course vary with differences in the social contest of state forms, individual ones of which may have a highly predominant social component, or a less predominant and yet strong majority on minority religious component. The differences in the role of Hinduism in Nepal and India are cases in point. The same would be true for Islam: in Afganistan state fundamentalism as taught by the Taliban; in Pakistan — the contemporary trend to divert attention from socio-economic or sectarian problems by attempts to construct a state religion with support from the Jamiat-Islami; in Bangladesh — contradictions between the forces of religiosity and secularism (as represented by the Awami League resuscitation); in India where resurgent Hindu ritualism seeks to browbeat the large Muslim minority and also now the Christian minority; and in Sri Lanka and Nepal where Islam is a small minority.

Justice for minorities was what M.A. Jinnah spoke of, though in an unjustifiably haughty tone arrogating 'sole spokesmanship' for the Islamic community in British India despite its many differences, at the time of the Congress governments in some provinces in 1937-39, and again during the Transfer of Power negotiations. But social justice was also what people by then quite opposed to Jinnah, like Maulana Azad, spoke of — for instance with regard to the federative principles of the Cabinet Mission Plan of 1946, which the Maulana clutched at like a straw of hope for an ultimately united India, and which Nehru and the Congress rejected, following on to the carnage of August '46 and after, which further embittered the late colonial communalist milieu. The rhetoric of justice for entire communities was certainly based on power and vote blocks. But was it based only on such stark secular principles?

A man like Jinnah could not have had very much Ulama support from the great U.P. Ulama centres such as Deoband or Lucknow or Azamgarh. Maulana Husain Ahmad Madani or Tufail Ahmad Manglauri, who had written '*Hindustani Musalmanon ka Raushan Mustakbil*', are cases in point. On the other hand, behind the Muslim League movement for Pakistan in 1940 onwards (when Jinnah led Muslim businessmen profiting from the British Indian war effort in deciding not to join the Congress in the latter's campaign not to forsake imperialist, as well as fascist, war, as a legitimate part of international relations) there was a lot of support from peasant leaders of the Indus Basin, acting as quartermasters for the British Indian Army — all the way from Gilgit, Chitral and Hazara to Sindh and Baluchistan, including the Punjab. This comes out from David Gilmartin's sound book on the Punjab landholding *Pirs* and the movement for Pakistan in the last years of British India.

But on the other hand, Sara Ansari's excellent book about Sindhi nationalism at the same time, shows Sindhi *Pirs* divided in their support for either Jinnah or clear anti-colonialism. In the then well-known instance of the *Pir* of Pagaro and the Hur movement he led, the Hurs were neither pro-league nor pro-War: they were anti-British leading to civil war in Sindh. This could be broken by its government only because the pro-establishment zamindars swung to the latter and after Pagaro was politically isolated, later to the League in the post-War crisis of British India. Let alone Khan Abdul Ghaffar Khan and his Khudai Khidmatgars of the Congress 'thrown to the wolves' in 1947—there were anti-colonial holy men fighting British incursions on Pathan tribal life in the North-West Frontier Province till the end of the Second World War; for instance the Haji of Turangzai, or most important, the *Fakir* of Ipi, conceptual ancestor of the Afghan Mujahideen today, whose valleys were bombed and strafed by British fighter planes, much as the Soviet bombed Panjshiris under Massoud, or the USA has rocket-targeted Khost (not too far from Ipi) in the name of punishing Osama bin Laden succoured by the Taliban. Religious fanaticism has political objectives, often localist, and nothing as fantastic as any 'civilisational faultliness' so dear to hardnosed diplomatic justification of'national interest' in international relations. One might speak of varieties of domestic Islam in which secular forces by no means lost the struggle to check political pietism.

When one thinks of domestic Islam, one is thinking of Sufi-influenced practices. Of course in the Panjab, such practices had become controlled by the 1940s by recruiters for the imperial army, paramilitary forces or canal colony labour. To Winston Churchill, chagrined by' the Congress revolt of 1942' in the Gangetic Plains and the heart of the Western Ghats, writing (as may be found in the Transfer of Power documents edited by Mansergh and Lumby) about the need to rely from henceforth for British imperial defence on the recruitment potential in the Panjab, religion was a lever to mobilise a manpower reservoir, where the rest of India leaked. To Postwar politicians in Britain, the younger brothers and nephews of the cannon fodder of the Punjab, whether Pakistanis from Jhang, Jhelum or occupied Kashmir or Indians from the Marjha or Malwa, became usable as cheap labour for rebuilding the bombed industrial areas of the Midlands, the Scots Lowlands and later the Home counties. These are factors beneath Pakistan and its aftermath in Punjab and Kashmir that should not be disregarded when they are seen only in terms of religion.

Are political power and modern religion necessarily exclusive, or is the Venn's diagram model of intersecting circles a better way of looking at it? Can we emphasise, as we have been doing collectively in the Indian History Congress since the 1960s, that power is what the politics of religion as well as secularism is all about? By adding the words 'Politics of' are we not narrowing down the scope of 'religion' in the human mind?

Let me take an example of how a secular viewpoint on Turkey has changed dimensions in the last half-century. As a boy — during the last days of the War-I read in the staunch Muslim, but quite secular Muslim household of the Ghuznavis of Saiyid Ameer Avenue in Calcutta, which welcomed me with open arms in my own troubled time, a dog-eared blue Penguin by a quite imperialist British writer H.C. Armstrong, called *Grey Wolf*, a biography of Ghazi Mustafa Kamal Ataturk. From these days, I remember Bengali Muslim pride in Turkish secularity. We heard also of Halide Edib, the avant-garde lady who had contacts with Congress in India in the 1930s. So, in 1959 when in Oxford as a PhD. student, I read about the way in which post-Inonu Turkey was changing back to religious ritualism, with rivulets of sacrificed goats' blood flowing in country town streets on *Id*, one felt that religions observances were necessarily reactionary. But in recent years, continuing to follow with interest, the revival of Islam as politics of freedom to worship or observe ritual in domestic life, and about varieties of conservatism represented by Turgut Ozal, Suleyman Demirel, Tansu Ciller, or Necmettin Erbakan, one doubts whether it is enough to think of public religious observance as merely the simple politics of power.

Not only in the most well-known case of Iran, but also in many countries, further east, pious morality in the form of public religiosity as a binding political force has come to mean a great deal in domestic politics. This applies to Buddhism in Sri Lanka, South-East Asian littoral as much as in Bhutanese state politics or Tibetan protest or Mongolian politics. It applies to Hinduism as a majoritarian force in India and Nepal. But it is not necessary to use Huntington's 'civilizational' absolutism to reify this as one form of social politics. Nor is it necessary, from an arid secularist position to wish away the fact that common religiosity can be potently mobilised as a religious force in electoral politics. Such mobilisation can lead to religious as well as politically fascist intolerance. Pietism can cloak it by appealing to middle class values. Islam, no less than Hinduism, Buddhism, or above all blatant Christianity of the Clinton-Blair variety bombing Saddam Husain in the name of unipolar powerful 'international community', or in 1999 bombing the Eastern Orthodox Serbians in the name of NATO security, can act as an oppressive force. If religion as the young Marx said is "the cry of the oppressed as well as the oppressor, it is the opium of the masses", it also constitutes a cat's cradle of sociability. It is for people to decide how particular stateforms of sociability are going to operate. What are the terms broader than 'civilisational' or 'religious' which define sociality?

This leads to my last point of qualification about the concept of Islam as a system of power or even of beliefs. Should we not have spent some time analysing the role played autonomously by language and the mental construction of reality, which changes from age to age. It is only scripturally that it is possible to define immutable eternity. I am in total agreement with Dr. Asghar Ali Engineer when he tells us that even here it is necessary to consider context in addition to text. Context after all includes concepts of change. There can be nothing immutable in change. Text can be supposed to be immutable by someone called 'x'. It is certain that'u','v' and 'w' will not have the view/s of immutability of 'x's predilection. And you can go on to the 'n'th degree on this matter. In terms of varieties of contact, language is a very important variable.

Certain geocultural elements in Islam have also to be considered as specificities in the construction of nationalism. What is always emphasised is the Arabian diaspora. Arabic cultures did develop in the Fertile Crescent and in North Africa and sub-Saharan Africa as well as across what the Arabs called al-Bahr al-Hind and only Europeans later called the Arabian Sea, leapfrogging from Zanzibar and the Maldives to South-West Sri-Lanka to Malaysia, Indonesia, Sabah and even a small minority in Cambodia. One would like wider information about the cultural base of Islam as it was based in the Sultanate of Acheh; for instance Islamic practice as studied by the Dutch scholar at the beginning of this century, Snouck-Hurgronje, on the piety of the popular anti-colonial front in Sumatra, the Sarekat Islam.

But apart from the Arab diaspora which South Asian Muslims by and large affiliate with, there is also a Turko-Iranian set of cultures, splayed out from Inner Asian China (Kansu, Ninghsia and Xinjiang with its predominance of Uighur Muslims) through the five Central Asian Republics of the CIS and Afghanistan and Northern Iran into the Caucasus up to Chechnya and Daghestan. The bosses of the arc that this represents are the mountain-linked cultures in the Caucasus, Elburz, Kopet Dagh, Pamir, Hindu Kush and Karakoram mountains, with Iranian and Turkic culture in collaboration as well as conflict in regions like the southern Caucasus foothills, or in Khorasan, Herat, Merv or Samarkand and Bukhara. The outer reaches of this culture may be found as far north-east as Kazan on the Volga, and southeast to Daulatabad in western Deccan in India, both extremes of the Mongol-Turko-Iranian ensemble of the Middle Ages, which Ibn Battuta visited in the course of the travels.

This cultural ensemble, diverse in its character, is quite distinct from Arabicate culture, but is as Islamic. Marshall Hodgson in his superb writings on Islamic historical sociology, speaks of Islamicate countries. I would like to add another element—the politics outside the pale of the old caliphates of Baghdad, Cairo and Morocco. In the late Medieval and Early Modern periods, the non-Arab dominated periphery split into Ottoman Khilafat-dominated, and non-Khilafati lands. It was only in the late nineteenth century that Pan-Islam and Jadidism began to be influential. These are divergences from even bipolar models —one can move from the Indic unity to South Asian diversity, from African compositeness to sub-Saharan variety, and so on. We know very little in Asia about the Islam of the Emirs of Kano, of the Tuaregs of the desert or the specifics of Sudanese fundamentalism defensively aggressive against its black subjects.

In all these countries, the situation is further variegated by alternative reactions to ruling colonialisms and to their neighbouring colonialists. The reactions in Anglophone countries are well-known in India. This is not the case with Francophone or Hollandophone lands. And you have a set of reactions about which we have heard nothing in the last two days—in the Russophone countries of CIS-Caucasia and Central Asia described by Bartold in his many books, which broke up between 1916 (the beginning of the revolt in Turkistan all the way from Dzhizhak near Samarkand to Semirechiye, of the local Sarts and Kyrgyz against Russian recruitment into its disastrous part in the First World War) and 1924 (when all frontiers there were changed by the formation of Republics under Stalin's Nationalities Law of that year). At a certain level, the Turkic language was stamped into domestic privacy by the Russian language and Islam of the mediterranean by Bolshevik atheism: to the extent that even today when Uzbek, the languagc of Bukhara, Tashkent or the Fergana towns is the state language of Uzbekistan, Russian a link language of the five Republics is as important as, say, English was in India in the 1950s. This linguistic confusion and loss of indigenous historical memory, but rejection of recent communist history, has led to new chauvinist identities. Amir Timur, Mirza Ulugh Beg, and even Babur whom the Uzbek Shaibani Khan actually drove out of Samarkand into Afghanistan, are all treated as heroes—even more than pre-Islamic ruling clans or Shaibani himself, the founder of the Uzbek dynasty, defeated by the Safavids of Iran, or the Bukhara Uzbek Mangit Khans who built the Registan in Samarkand. Contact with the broader aspects of Turco-Iranian culture through Imam Bukhari, Ahmad al-

Fergani, Ali Sher Navoi and the Herat efflorescence under the Timurids is now claimed as Uzbek identity. These new concepts of identity, give specificity to nationalism as it develops in Islamic countries, and the modern character of language-forms give particular imprint to these specificities.

So to sum up, diversity as socially and scientifically is more important than the absolutist concept of just 'religion' in understanding Islam as a continuing force. The more it changes, it is not necessarily the same thing! It may be worthwhile to look at religion as a unity if one wishes to do so, that is if one is so spiritually inclined. But it is also worthwhile as historians and/or social scientists to look at the social diversity which religious labels encapsulate.

Endnotes:

1. Syeda Saiyidain Hameed, *India's Maulana, Abul Kalam Azad, Centenary Volume II, Selected Speeches and Writings of Maulana Abul Kalam Azad* (Indian Council for Cultural Relations, and Vikas Publishing House, New Delhi, 1990) and Syeda Saiyidain Hameed, *Islamic Seal on India's Independence. Abul Kalam Azad - A Fresh Look* (Oxford University Press, Karachi, 1998).
2. *India's Maulana. op. cit.* pp. 49-57 (a selection made by the editor herself).
3. Ian Henderson Douglas, Abul Kalam Azad, *An Intellectual and Religious Biography* (ed. By Gall Minault and Christian W. Troll, Oxford University Press, Delhi 1988) and V.N. Datta, Maulana Azad (Manohar Publication, 1990).
4. All quotations from this speech are taken from the abbreviated version available in *India's Maulana*, II, pp. 135-36 and 145-46.
5. *i.e. mleccha*, a term used by Sanskritising Hindus to disparage mainly Muslims and Christians as'impure'.
6. Explicated in Barun De,'Introduction: A Mirror Crack'd from Side to Side—Colonialism, Class, Caste and Communalism' in Sekhar

Bandopadhyay, Suranjan Das (Editors) *Caste and Communal Politics in South Asia* (K.P. Bagchi, Calcutta, 1993) pp. 1-28.

7. *India's Maulana.* II. P. 146.
8. In November 1922, the Turks deposed the Sultan Caliph and made Abdul Majid the nominal Khalifa with no temporal powers. In October 1923, the Grand National Assembly declared Turkey a Republic and exiled Abdul Majid. The Khilafat was abolished in March, 1924' Syeda Saiyidain Hameed, *Islamic Seal on India's Independence. Abul Kalam Azad - A Fresh Look*, op. cit. 139.
9. *India's Maulana* II, op.cit. p. 49.
10. *ibid*, p. 51.
11. *ibid*, p. 52.
12. *ibid*, p. 53.
13. *ibid*, p. 55.
14. *ibid*, p. 56.
15. Latest reference, Barun De, 'Imperialism, Nationalism and the Dialectics of Changing Identity in the Indian Subcontinent' in Joachim Heidrich, ed. *Changing Identities, the Transformation of Asian and African Societies under Colonialism* (Centre for Modern Oriental Studies, Berlin, Studies 1, 1994).
16. *ibid*, p. 53.
17. *ibid*, p. 55.
18. *ibid*, p. 56.
19. *India's Maulana* II, p. 56.

Indian Response to Islam

D.R. Goyal

India is home to the second largest segment of the followers of Islam although it is not counted among the family of Muslim or Islamic states. And yet it is not, would not like to be, an anti-Islamic or anti-Muslim society or state. Most Indians do not subscribe to the view that civilisations unavoidably clash or that Islam represents essentially an aggressive, combative civilisation incapable of coexistence with civilisations built around other faiths.

It would however be erroneous to claim that India's response to Islam has been uniformly positive. It is indeed unrealistic to expect uniformity of response from a country of continental proportions, having almost unprecedented climatic and cultural variety. Its vast alluvial planes and network of rivers combined to make it a land of comfort and plenty, a congenial place for settled and peaceful life. It was a perennial attraction for outsiders seeking fortune as its own inhabitants were loath to travel abroad on account of religio-social restrictions against venturing beyond the boundaries defined by high mountains in the north and sea in east, south and west. The responses to the influences from abroad were determined by the motivations and behaviour of the immigrants.

India's interaction with Islam started from its very inception. In the intervening fourteen centuries the responses have varied according to the behaviour and conduct of its followers, whether outsiders or local converts. Contemporary perceptions of Islam and Muslims, particularly among some sections of non-Muslim Indians, are the direct outcome of the interface between the two but significantly influenced by the imperialist British rule.

The partition of the country and establishment of avowedly Islamic state in a part of the landmass is the result of the British policy pursued for two centuries. The British rulers believed that the stability of their rule depended upon conflict between major religious communities, the Hindus and the Muslims. They directed their administrative and cultural policies to accentuate differences through interpretation of medieval Indian history as a period of continuous confrontation between the two. Those who developed aversion to the British rule saw through the game and began to stress commonness of interests and the essential unity of religions.

Thus developed two kinds of responses of essential divergence and fundamental convergence which are reflected in two different approaches to nationhood:

(i) common nationhood based on freedom of religion and commonness of secular interests and,

(ii) two nations, one Hindu and the other Muslim.

Traces of both can be witnessed even today, more of the former kind in India and the latter in Pakistan. Free India's Constitution ensuring equality of citizenship, freedom of conscience and protection of religio-cultural identities of minority communities, including Muslims, highlights India's response to Islam. It is noteworthy that it was adopted after the formation of a separate state, Pakistan, which called itself Islamic.

The idea of common nationhood was developed and shared by all Indians irrespective of religious affiliation. Eminent Muslim scholars and divines made a significant contribution to the development of this concept even as they actively participated in the struggle against British colonialism. Hindus on the other hand shared the outrage of Muslims when European powers meted out unjust treatment to the Muslim world. Khilafat and non-cooperation movements are outstanding examples of that. So is the consistent Indian support to the Palestine cause.

Maulana Abul Kalam Azad, for example, held the view:

> "Islam has now as great a claim on the soil of India as Hinduism. If Hinduism has been the religion of the people here for several thousands of years, Islam also has been their religion for a thousand years. Just as a Hindu can declare with pride that he is an Indian and follows Hinduism, so also can we say with equal pride that we are Indians and we follow Islam. I shall enlarge this orbit still further. The Indian Christian is equally entitled to say with pride that he is an Indian and he is following a religion of India, namely, Christianity."

In the context of Hindu-Muslim relations he laid the greatest emphasis on harmony between the two, saying that without it all hope of independence, survival and progress of the country would be an idle dream. Without it not only will it be impossible to attain national independence but we shall fail to develop in ourselves the basic attributes and values of humanity. "Therefore even if an angel descends from high heavens and proclaims from top of the Qutub Minar that Swaraj would come within 24 hours if we renounce the goal of Hindu-Muslim unity my response would be to renounce Swaraj but not unity. Because, if Swaraj is delayed, it would be loss only of India but if we lose unity it would be a loss for entire humanity," he declared.

Two Nation Theory

The spearhead of common nationhood and harmony among religions was Mahatma Gandhi. His response to religion-centred nationalism or the so-called 'two nation theory' was: "The 'two nations' theory is an untruth. The vast majority of Muslims of India are converts to Islam or are the descendents of converts. They did not become a separate nation, as soon as they became converts. A Bengali Muslim speaks the same tongue that a Bengali Hindu does, eats the same food and has the same amusements, as his Hindu neighbour. They dress alike. I have often found it difficult to distinguish by outward sign, between a Bengali Hindu and a Bengali Muslim. The same phenomenon is observable more or less in the south among the poor who constitute the masses of India.

> "When I first met the late Sir Ali Imam, I did not know that he was not a Hindu. His speech, his dress, his manners, his food were the same as of the majority of the Hindus in whose midst I found him. His name alone betrayed him. Not even that with Qaid-e-Azam Jinnah. For his name could be that of any Hindu. When I first met him, I did not know that he was a Muslim. I came to know his religion,

> when I had his full name given to me. His nationality was written in his face and in his manner. The reader will be surprised to know that for days, if not months, I used to think of the late Vithalbhai Patel as a Muslim, as he used to sport a beard and a Turkish cap. The Hindu law of inheritance governs many Muslim groups. Sir Mahomed Iqbal used to speak with pride of his Brahminical descent. Iqbal and Kitchlew are names common to Hindus and Muslims. Hindus and Muslims of India are not two nations. Those whom God has made one, man will never be able to divide."

That is the best testimony of how harmoniously the two civilisations commingled and interpenetrated. Gandhi's views were endorsed by leading Islamic intellectuals of the time.

In one of his lectures Sir Sayyid thus exhorted his Muslim audience:

> "We came into this country even as did the enlightened communities of Hindus. Hindus forgot about the land of their origin and their period of migration and made this country their homeland. They recognised this land between the Himalayas and the Vindhyachal as their homeland. We also left our land centuries ago. We have no memories of those climates, the beauty of those environments; the freshness and taste of those fruits. Nor do we remember the blessings of the holy land of sands and stones. We too adopted this as our homeland and made it our abode. Thus, Hindostan alone is the homeland of both. We breathe the air of Hindostan and eat its food. We are sharers in life and death.

> Our blood has undergone transformation through intermingling and our complexions and appearances have developed similarity. The Mussalmans have adopted several Hindu customs even as the Hindus have taken to Muslim habits. So much so that our interaction has created a new language, Urdu, which was neither our language nor theirs.
>
> "So, if we ignore that aspect of our being which is related to God we are one nation as inhabitants of this land. Progress and welfare of the country as well as of both of us, therefore, is possible through unity, mutual sympathy and love. On the other hand disunity and ill will will destroy both. Woe to those who do not understand this and seek to promote differences between the two communities for they do not realise that they would themselves be the victims of its disastrous consequences; they inflict injury on themselves."

Maulana Hussain Ahmad Madni similarly stressed the commonness of interests between various communities and wrote:

> "Who can deny that whatever difference there be among them on issues of religion they are stringed together as Hindostanis (Indians). This relationship makes their interests common. As Indians whatever is good for a Hindu is good for a Mussalman and what is harmful for the Mussalman is inevitably harmful for the Hindu. Thus their nation and nationhood is the same."

These ideas reflect the authentic Indian response to Islam and of its true followers to India. As a result of this interaction has developed an ethos which we have inherited and which is embodied in our Constitution. There is a common nationhood and a common culture and a never-dying desire to cooperate with all neighbours.

It is noteworthy that both aggressiveness of Islam and hostility towards it has been manifested more in North India than in the south. The movement for a separate state for Muslims also had bulk of its adherents in the northern states. In discussions on communal relations in the south one often comes across a comment.' It is a product of north India'.

Like every ideology Islam has two aspects: one, spiritual upliftment enabling human beings to establish better and harmonious relations with others, and two, power which enables some to dominate others. The former carries the messages of love, equality and oneness of humanity and the latter makes a distinction of high and low treating the vanquished as inferior, unworthy of equal treatment. One attracts, the other repels.

Northern and Southern Perceptions

The differences in southern and northern perceptions is the result of the circumstances and the form in which Islam entered. While in the south it was introduced by Arab traders, who had been carrying on their trading activities long before the birth of Islam contributing to prosperity of local inhabitants, in the north it had a hostile visage for it came in the wake of conquering and marauding hoards of Afghans, Turks and Mughals.

Scholars testify that Arab traders had been active on the coastal regions of India for a long time and were treated with respect on account of their fair dealings and their contribution to the economic prosperity of the territories in which they operated. When they brought the message of Islam it was received with respect and reverence. Islam appeared with its simple, well defined beliefs and practices and democratic approach to social organisation and influenced the whole atmosphere. By 9th century it was adopted by the ruler of Cannanore, Cheraman Perumal. He and his descendant the rulers of Malabar, the Zamorin, gave all facilities for construction of mosques and spread of Islam. Arab traders made considerable contribution not only to trade and commerce but also in the campaign of Zamorin for territorial expansion. The reverence in which they were held is apparent from the appellation 'Mapillal (Moplah) used for them. It means 'distinguished boy' or bridegroom. The Muslims enjoyed high social status.

While this process was on, Islam got introduced in the north-western territory of Sind with the conquest of Sind by Mohammed Bin Qasim. But it did not evoke any hostile reaction partly because the Arab rulers did not show disrespect to local beliefs and traditions. It is said that Khalifa Omar had reprimanded some of his sea-faring soldiers for misbehaviour towards others and issued strict orders to pay due respect to other people's ideas, customs and traditions. The Hindus of Sind were recognised and respected as believers. When Mohammed Bin Qasim wrote to the Khalifa in Damascus that the Hindus worshipped cow the latter issued orders prohibiting cow-slaughter not only in Sind but also throughout the territory under his influence. Sind became the main channel of transmission of Hindu scientific and philosophical thoughts to Baghdad. Books by Brahmagupta, Charak and Susruta on medicine, pharmacology and toxicology were translated into Arabic. Royal physician to Harun-al-Rashid was a Hindu. Many Arab scholars travelled to Sind and took Sanskrit scholars back to Baghdad. There they translated hundreds of Sanskrit books on mathematics, astronomy, astrology, music etc. into Arabic. The scholars were paid handsome fees and repatriated to their homes without being forced to embrace Islam. As a result of this enlightened attitude, 60 per cent Hindus voluntarily embraced Islam in Sind.

In sharp contrast to this, stands the next phase of Hindu-Muslim contact when Turko-Afghan and Mughal invaders came and established their rule. They were actuated more by economic and worldly motives than by disinterested religious zeal. The Ghaznis, Ghoris, Khiljis, Mughals, Timur, Nadir Shah, etc. came to India for worldly gains. They were not motivated by the missionary spirit of Islam. They set up their administration and ruled firmly over many parts of India for more than seven hundred years and yet India does not contain even a bare majority of Muslims. The rulers were Muslim, the rule was not Islamic.

Aggressive Face of Muslim Invaders

The aggressive face of Islam starts from Mahmood Ghaznavi. Mahmood Ghaznavi and Mohammad Ghauri and later conquerors were not as benign as Mohammad Bin Qasim. It would be wrong to say that they did not commit any offence. We will be flying in the face of history if we deny that quite a number of temples were destroyed. In medieval times, destruction of the vanquished peoples' place of worship was a way of asserting sovereignty. This had been done not only by Muslims but also pre-Muslim rulers whether they were Buddhist or Vaishnavite or Shaivait. They have been destroying each other's temples. So, these Muslims from Afghanistan or beyond also indulged in that practice of asserting their sovereignty.

At the same time, these new conquerors found themselves in a situation where they realised that it was impossible to eliminate all those who followed a different religion but inhabited this land. This realisation acted as a curb on what may be called the proselytising zeal which eventually gave way to the practical considerations of governance. And then started what may be called the period of peaceful co-existence of which Ibn Batuta talked in his memoirs. There are several authoritative accounts which establish that they not only tolerated the religion of the vanquished people but also tried to incorporate their talents into their governance. High posts, both in army and civil administration, particularly in revenue department, were given to non-Muslims. The only people who protested against this were the 'Ulema who had come with these conquerors. They were occasionally administered snubs.

Now this confluence during the period of tolerant co-existence led to the developments which today we see manifest in literature, art, architecture, and painting, creative work of high aesthetic value which is a part of India's proud heritage.

It must also be asserted that the conversions to Islam were less because of force or power or even political patronage. It is the Sufis who made Islam attractive to common people. Especially to those who had been suffering humiliating discrimination at the hands of orthodox Hindus. If we look around at Muslim colonies in various parts of the country, we will find that they are generally around the centres of

Sufi order. It is the conduct of the Sufis, their humanitarian, compassionate approach to human life and living that evoked warm response from people; and they never insisted on conversion. Nizamuddin Aulia, for instance remarked that every community has its own object of worship.

Process of Synthesis

Interaction of religions during the Medieval Period to a process of synthesis of the two civilisations in the form of Sufi and Bhakti movements. Hindu religions were monotheistic at their core; but they had acquired a polytheistic appearance on account of popular mythology. The severe *tawhid* of Islam enabled Hindus to retrieve their original monotheistic position. The Bhakti movement and the Sikh Panth were direct products of Hindu-Muslim interaction. Hindus became less exclusive and admitted non-Hindus in their religious fold after the 14th century. Muslim Sufis borrowed the disciplines of *asanas* (physical postures), *prannyam* (breath control) and *dhyan* (concentrated meditation) from Hindu *jogis.* Caste system proved tenacious and resisted Islamic equality. Indeed, it penetrated the Muslim communities also.

Muslims of India have made significant contribution even to Islamic thought. Shah Waliyullah of Delhi, a towering personality of the 18th century served as a beacon of light for the evolution of religious thoughts of Islam. According to him economic equity was essential for the cultural development of mankind. A state did not become Islamic, he said, merely because it was governed by a Muslim ruler. On the other hand, he asserted, a state could be called Islamic even if it was governed by a just non-Muslim ruler.

He can thus be described as the initiator of the ideas that found culmination in the approach to nationhood advocated by Gandhi and Abul Kalam Azad. The revolutionary ideas of Shah Waliyullah were disliked by agents of the British East India Company and attempt was made to physically eliminate him which fortunately did not succeed. Then a concerted effort was made to paint him as a fanatic agent of pan-Islamism or hegemonist Islam.

This process of confluence got disrupted during the British period which cannot be ignored. Even though the significance of, British policy of divide and rule in this context is sometimes sought to be underestimated as a stale old cliche the fact cannot be denied. That policy led to what may be called conflictual relationships between some followers of Islam and some followers of Hinduism. 'Some' because the response was confined or articulated by the elite of both communities who were concentrated in urban areas. They were interested more in getting jobs and concessions. Therefore, they were interested more in currying favour with the alien rule and it was the competition for currying favour that created the phenomena that we call communalism.

Islamic Approaches to Nationhood and Nation Building

Asghar Ali Engineer

Islam and nation and nation building is again a highly controversial subject. In fact, the concept of a nation is a very modern concept — one can say 18th century concept. Such a concept never existed when the holy Prophet of Islam was preaching. So, it is difficult to find something in original sources that what was the position of Islam as far as nation is concerned. But there are certain things which can act as our guide even if we are inclined to accept the concept of nation in Islam. Now generally it is maintained that Islam is an international religion and the concept of Muslim Umma is not confined to any territory; and nation is basically a territorial concept. Many Islamic thinkers find contradiction in Islam and nationhood. Nationhood is alien to Islam, they maintain.

Another thing is the belief that there is no separation of politics and religion in Islam. Now if such positions are taken, then there will be lot of problems in accepting nationhood. But there are other things. One thing is that we can never understand any text without its context. A text must be placed in its context then only the text yields meaning. There may be certain aspects of the text which are transcendental and so transcendental aspects should be separated from the contextual aspects, or what we can say we must distinguish between normative and contextual. Unfortunately, this is not done often and this leads to a lot of controversy and also a lot of confusion and many questions arise. Even conflictual situations develop. In the modern context we have to re-read the text. By text, means both the holy Qur'an as well as *hadith*. There are people who would not like to re-read it. That itself would be considered a sinful act by many theologians. Now if all agree to re-read and situate our text in our context, then there are obvious guidelines in the text also for accepting nationhood.

Khilafat and *Imamat*

Now even in the early history of Islam, the differences arose. For example, at one time it was maintained that there can be only one Khalifa. Of course, the other controversy was between Shias and Sunnis of Immamah and *Khalifa*. Shias believe that the Imam has to be there to guide the community and Imam is appointed by *Nass* and it is *ilham min Allah*. *Naṣṣ* is done through *ilham min Allah*, that is, inspiration from God. And, Sunnis maintain that the Prophet did not leave any such concept and it is Umma which will elect the *Khalifa*. This was one controversy. Another controversy in Sunni Islam was about *Khalifa*. At one time, it was maintained that there can be only one *Khalifa*. But when Ummayads were overthrown and Abbasis took over and in Spain another Ummayad *Khilafat* was established, there was controversy that how can there be two *Khalifa* at a time and who will be accepted as the authentic *Khalif*. But then political theorists in Islam at that time accepted the concept of two *Khalifas* and subsequently there were more. The Fatmis established their Khilafat in Egypt, Spain and in other parts of Africa and the Islamic world. Number of rulers came into existence. So, again the theory had to be modified. There has been no single political theory which had universal acceptance. There were controversies in early history of Islam. Even concept of *Umma*, for example, if we take *Misaqe Madina*, that is the covenant of Madina, which Holy Prophet drew up with the help of religious leaders of other communities, It is very interesting. The situation in Madina was pluralistic, there was no single community. Muslims had just entered that city. Then there were tribals with their own religion. Then there were Jews and at a little distance from Madina there were some Christians also. So, the Holy Prophet drew up this covenant with leaders of different religions and it was known as *Misaqe Madina*. And it has very close parallel to the Indian situation. That is why our leaders of Jamiyatul Ulama, Maulana Hussain Ahmad Madani in particular, gave example of *Misaqe Madina* to counter two nation theory, because Jinnah by then had propounded his two-nation theory. The resolution was not adopted but the discussion was in the air and Maulana Hussain Ahmad Madani gave example of *Misaqe Madina* that when the Holy Prophet could accept plurality and give full freedom to the followers of all religions including tribal religion where there was no question of book. In case of Jews and in case of Christians there was a book but as far as the tribals were concerned who had not accepted any religion of the book, they were also given freedom to practice their religion. *Misaqe Madina* can become our guide if we are prepared to re-read the text. And there even the concept of *Umma* was very different. It was not Muslim community but it was *Madinese community*; all were included; Jews were included; tribals were included and Muslims were included. The concept of *Umma* in Madina was very different from its later meaning which confined only to Muslim later on. But as far as the Holy Prophet was concerned, he did not confine it to the Muslims alone.

Qur'an and Pluralism

Then Qur'an also has certain verses which strongly emphasise pluralist situation. One is, of course, which we Muslims recite in our daily prayers:

> Tell, oh Prophet that *kafirs* have their way of worship and I have my way of worshipping. I will never worship the way the *kafirs* worship and they will never worship the way I worship. And *lakum dinakum wa liyadin* that is, for you is your religion and for me is my religion.

So, that is also a pluralistic text. Another text which is more clear in this respect is:

> If Allah wanted, He could have created one *Umma*, one community. But he did not do so in order to test you. Whether you can live in peace and harmony in a pluralist situation. *Le yabluwakum fi ma ātākum* - what is given to us is pluralist situation, *fastabiwuIkhhagrat* and the real thing is excel each other in good deeds.

The whole emphasis is on this. Again *likullin wijhatun huwa muwalliha*—that for each there is a way, there is a direction in which one turns and worships. But the real thing is *Istabaq bill khairat* — that is, excellence in good deeds. The emphasis is on this. Now if this becomes our guideline, then the pluralist situation in India or in any nation for that matter will be there. Because today, there is no nation in the world which is not pluralistic because of faster means of communication. We can reach America in 18 hours or we can reach England in 8 hours. Distances have shortened that way and people are going and settling in different countries for earning their livelihood or for better prospects. So, all countries, all nations have become pluralistic and pluralism has to be accepted. Rejection of pluralism today in any process of nation building can cause very severe problems. That was realised by the Ulama in India also. It is very interesting to note that the two-nation theory was propounded by a modernist, not by a theologian. Jinnah was a modernist. He had nothing to do with Islam, he could not even recite Holy Qur'an. He had no initiation in Islamic studies at all. He did not know basic elements of Islam. He was trained in a Western university. He could speak only English. He could not speak even his own mother tongue. So a modernist propounded the two nation theory because it was all about power struggle between the elites of two communities. It had nothing to do with religion or religious concept. The controversy in reality was not whether Islam permits Muslims to live in this country or whether justice is being done to Muslims. These are the two very different things. Jinnah's whole conflict was about certain share in power. If that had been given to Muslims, he would have happily accepted co-existence in India. In fact, until 1928, Jinnah was advocating united India. When Motilal Nehru Committee Report came, Jinnah said in his speech with folded hands, please accept Muslim demand for one-third share in power in Parliament. If you accept that, India will remain united. And he posed the question: "Don't you want India to remain united? Please accept this demand and I will persuade Muslim leaders to accept joint electorate." Now until 1928, he was talking of joint electorate. It was only after 1937 the situation changed when Jinnah came out with the concept of two nations. And his whole theory of two-nation neither stood the test of religious teachings nor of sociological reality in India because the examples which he gave, the arguments which Jinnah advanced, they can be torn to pieces by any sociologist or by any political scientists. Those arguments were not valid arguments. Yet the situation was such that, unfortunately, it became acceptable to the Muslim elite and ultimately our country was divided. But all Ulama of prominence stood by nationalism. And Maulana Husain Ahmad Madani not only stood by nationalism but he campaigned for nationalism very actively. He started his campaign from Assam and went right up to south persuading Muslims not to accept the two-nation theory. He even wrote a book *Muttaheda Qaumiyat Aur Islam.* And he proves from Qur'anic verses that *kafirs* and prophets always shared territorial nationality. That was his argument. And he quoted verse after verse from Holy Qur'an to show that Prophets and unbelievers always shared nationality. There was no difference of nationality. They were from the same *Qau'm* (community) and yet they followed different religions. Then of course, he gave the example of *Misaqe Madina.* So this is a very important aspect of Islam that it accepts pluralism. That is why, Qur'an maintained that we have not brought any new truth. We confirm the truth which was sent earlier. *Mussadiqan ma bayna yadayn* — we have come to confirm the truth which is there, which is before us. That was the statement of the Qur'an and that is why, The Qur'an also said that you have to accept all the Prophets. And those who do not accept all the Prophets, they are *kafirs*, they are not Mumin; a Mumin has to accept all the Prophets.

Territorial Nationhood in Islam

This was extended to other communities because the list of Prophets given in Holy Qur'an is illustrative, not exhaustive. And Muslims believe that there were one lakh twenty-four thousand Prophets. That is why, our Sufi saints thought that may be, Ram and Krishna who are so highly respected in India were also perhaps prophets of God because how could Allah forget this great country and would not send his Prophets here. All these arguments enable us to accept the concept of nationhood, which is territorial. Now Maulana Hussain Ahmed Madani also argued that we must make distinction between *Qaum* and *millat. Millat* is international as far as Muslims are concerned and *Qaum* is a territorial concept, a limited concept. So, Hindus and Muslims can be one *Qaum*, not in religious sense but in territorial sense. So, they can share nationality with non-Muslims whereas they will share their religion with their sisters and brothers throughout the world. He gave example, "if I go to Mecca, I will be greatly welcomed by my Muslim brothers there. But for how long? I can stay for six months, for one year, for two years. Thereafter they will say, well, you hold Indian passport. Thank you very much and go back". He has given this argument.

Millat and *Qaum* are two different concepts, two different entities which we must accept. Both have equal validity. Not that one has greater validity than the other. Even in Medieval Ages, *Umma* was broken politically into several empires. So why not in modern times? Modern conditions make it more compulsive for us to accept the concept of territorial entity. The same thing happened with Communism.

Now Communists talked of workers international and they

also rejected the concept of nation. But right in the beginning they were divided into China and Russia and they were at each other's throat. We know the whole history that Russia could not accept Chinese Communism and China could never accept Russian Communism. And always their borders were tense, they were fighting against each other. So, internationalism has its own validity. It might remain a dream that the entire humanity should be one but then Qur'an very realistically accepts both the positions.

Qur'an talks of *wa karramna bani i.e.* Adam. We have honoured the children of Adam which includes everybody. No one is excluded. But at the same time, it also says that we have created you, different tribes and different nationalities so that you may be recognised. That means, Quran's position is very realistic that it talks of internationalism also, of entire humanity also. But it talks of different identities as well. After all, you belong to different tribes, you belong to different nations, and you have different identities. And these identities should not conflict. They must co-exist harmoniously. This is the biggest problem in India today. Though we are one nation, but casteism, tribalism, regionalism and communalism—these are the conflicts of our times. What is happening in North-East? What is happening in Kashmir? What is happening between Hindus and Muslims? These problems are there. But if we really go by the Quran's teachings or for that matter Upnishadic teachings, we would not be fighting like this, we would be respecting each other's identities. Hindus should respect Muslim identity and Muslim should respect Hindu identity or ethnic identities and caste identities also. We should respect each other. But that requires justice. If we accept Muslim identity but do not give Muslim's due then conflicts will arise. Identity will be used for mobilisation. If we do not give Dalits their due but accept them, the conflict will arise. So it is not only identity, it is also justice. So, when we talk of the process of nation building, concept of justice becomes very important. That a few people in the country belonging to certain religious or regional or caste identity, monopolise all the power and resources, or if they monopolise all economic resources, and then they say we respect all other identities, this position will not be there. That is why, Jinnah is the best example. Because Muslim elites thought that justice was not done to them and power was not being shared with them. And in independent India, they would not be given justice, they would not be given their due. Jinnah came out with the two-nation theory. That is why, I say, the whole struggle was power oriented.

It was not religion oriented struggle. That is why, figures like Maulana Hussain Ahmed Madani had to clarify Islamic position. So all the eminent Ulama in India stood by the Congress or composite nationalism. Jinnah found it extremely difficult to get any *Aalim* of prominence to support this two-nation theory. Only Maulana Shabbir Ahmed Usmani did. But again, not because he was convinced of religious position but he had a fight in Jamatul Ulama and he left Jamatul Ulama and then began supporting Jinnah. Otherwise, Jinnah did not find a single *Aalim* of note to support his theory of two nations. That is why, I would like to clear this position in the minds of non-Muslims and also some Muslims that the two-nation theory was Islamic in any sense because Pakistan is going through a severe crisis today. If religion could unite people politically, this kind of crises would not have arisen in Pakistan.

What happened or what is happening in Pakistan clearly

shows that religious unity cannot translate into political unity. Now if we are aware of this fact that religious unity does not translate into political unity, our political behaviour would be very different. That time, many Muslims were misled and they thought religious unity translates into political unity. It does not. It is Pakistan which has broken into two pieces which had a religious state whereas India is still united which is a secular state. Because when all citizens have this sense of being equal citizens, other conflicts would remain whether they are getting due share or not, but if they are convinced of equal citizenship, they would not like to disturb it. But despite all persons following same religion, if they do not have a sense of equal citizenship, they are likely to break. That is why, Pakistan broke.

So, Islam does not in any way encourage political unity on the basis of religion and it has never existed in entire Islamic history. Political unity broke immediately after the death of the Holy Prophet. So there is no question that 1400 years after his death, there will be political unity. There was political unity only in his lifetime. But after his death, Muslims differed from each other politically and different political power centres came into existence. So, modern nationalism which is territorial in concept does not conflict with the basic teachings of Islam as long as we separate religious unity from political unity.

A Synthesis of Indo-Islamic Culture and the Role of Muslim Women

Zeenat Shaukat Ali

Annemarie Schimmel in her article on Islamic Spirituality in India says: "If one is interested in the history of religion, one may perhaps think of the Vedic Upanishads, regarded as the highest expression of wisdom ever since their Latin translation by Anquetil-Duperron appeared in 1801. But few people would know... that the Persian translation of the Upanishads on which Anquetie-Duperron based his work was made by Dara Shikoh, the mystical minded heir apparent of the Mughal empire"[1].

"The history of this heritage begins as early as 92/711, when a small contingent of Arabs under Muhammad ibn al-Qasim conquered the Sind, the southern part of present-day Pakistan, extending Muslim rule to Multan. The new province had to deal with a great number of Buddhist and Hindu citizens who were treated by Muhammad as *ahl al-kitab* (people of the book), like the Christians and Jews in the Near East."[2] He also established friendly relations between several Hindu leaders like the Solankis in Gujrat, Chauhans in Ajmer, Tomars in Delhi, Pawars in Malwa, Parihas in Kanauj and Palas in Bengal.

The establishment of Turkish rule in India opened up many opportunities for contact between Hinduism and Islam. Sind and Multan became a way station through which Indian mathematics, astronomy, and medicine reached the central parts of the Muslim world. The study of religious literature seems to have been popular among the Muslim scholars in the first capital of Sind.

Al-Beruni (*d.* after 1050) took the trouble to translate Sanskrit classics into Arabic. He then wrote his monumental *Kitab fi tahqiq ma li l-Hind* in order to acquaint his Ghaznavid rulers with Hinduism. He claimed that barriers separating Hindus from Muslims were based either on lack of education, political reasons or on language.

Al-Beruni's thesis is that "the beliefs of the educated and uneducated people differ in every nation" and that the "educated strive to conceive abstract ideas and to define general principles", while the uneducated submit to derived rules and regulations. Such a dichotomy applies to both religion and science. Discussing the concept of God, Al-Beruni says that Hindus believe "He is eternal, without beginning or end, acting by free will, almighty, all wise, living and giving life, ruling, preserving, one who is in His sovereignity is unique, beyond all likeness and unlikeness".[3] He quotes from Patanjali's, *Yog-Sutra, Bhagvat Gita* and the *Sankhya-Karika* to substantiate this assertion."

Akbar's translation bureau or the *Maktab Khana* helped gain an insight into the intellectual perception of Hinduism. Its most remarkable productions were the translations of the *Mahabharata*, the *Ramayana* and the *Yoga Vashishta.* Abul Fazl wrote the preface to the *Mahabharat.*[4] Discussing Akbar's motives for ordering the translations, he claimed that the

Emperor sought to heal the religious differences amongst his subjects. Akbar did not discriminate between Hindus and Muslims, friend and foe. He felt that reliably translated text from both religions would form a basis for a united search for truth.

In the third volume of the *A'in-i Akbari*, Abul Fazl gave a detailed description of Hinduism. He urged his Muslim readers to study his account of Hindu learning with open minds. He suggested that 'putting aside the estrangements of ignorance' they compare it with the religious teachings of the Sufis and the philosophers. The *A'in-i Akbari* includes some discussion on contemporary Hindu and Jain philosophy. Abul Fazl was amazed at the flexibility of *yogic* postures and interestedly described the Hindu knowledge of *Sakuna* (augury). Sanskrit works were also translated into Persian during Jehangir's reign.[5] During the sixteenth and seventeenth centuries, the Mujaddid (Shaykh Ahmad Sirhindi, 1564-1624) also considered that Prophets had come to India, and though some Muslims contradicted this, others supported his view. For instance, Mirza Mazhar Jan-i Janan (*d.* 1781), a distinguished Sufi scholar of the Mujaddids' Sufic order, accepted both Rama and Krishna as Prophets"[6]

Muslim Scholars and India

Rizwi in his historical thesis *On the Wonder that was India* reveals how Muslim men of learning were deeply impressed by India. For instance Amir Khusrau was impressed by the depth of learning among Indians, and their ability to speak any language. He also greatly admired the *Brahmans*, who could teach all subjects without having to study overseas and who had devised the numerical system, written *Kalila*

Wa Dinzna, a Persian translation of *Panchtantra* written in Sanskrit. These are stories based on morals, and invented chess.[7] Nakhshabi, who had translated two Sanskrit works, had a better understanding of Sanskrit. Mir Gisu Daraz also studied Sanskrit. Following his conquest of Nagarkot in 1362 Firuz Shah Tughlaq acquired some 1,300 books from Jwalamukhi temple. He commissioned Sanskrit scholars to translate some of them into Persian. On the basis of the translations of works on physics and astronomy, "Izzu'd-Din Khalid Khani compiled the *Dala-i Firuz Shahi*, a work that is not now available. One of the surviving Persian translations from Sanskrit is the *Bhratsamhita* by the celebrated Indian astronomer Varhamihira. It had been translated earlier by Al-Beruni, but the new translator, 'Abdul Aziz Shams Baha-i Nuri, does not seem to have had access to this work. Sultan Zaynul-Abidin of Kashmir, Sultan Sikandar Lodi, and several other Muslim rulers also ordered the translation of various Sanskrit works into Persian in order both to satisfy their own intellectual curiosity and to increase Muslim understanding of Hinduism.[8]

The unique synthesis of the Hindu Muslim cultures has sometimes been ignored or under represented. As Akbar Ahmed in his '*Living Islam*' points out, the best recent book on the Urdu poet Mirza Ghalib was produced not by a Muslim but by Pavan Varma, a bright young Indian diplomat, who is a Hindu (and currently Press Secretary to the President). It is a well-written sensitive and balanced account (*see* Varma, 1989).[9] But it hints at two things in contemporary India; that the strand of synthesis survives and is valued, but perhaps also that Muslims have lost the capacity, even to represent their own great figures. Newspaper articles and letters constantly cite Aurangzeb as a hero among some

Muslims but a villain for most Hindus. Few mention that on the whole Muslims were sensitive to their Hindu compatriots. From the start Babar abolished cow slaughter and up to the last Mughal emperor it was banned in Delhi as a gesture towards the Hindus; Sir Sayyed did the same in Aligarh.'[10]

Few know that Aurangzeb bestowed on the temple at Chitrakoot 200 bighas of land or that he gave the Jangambadi Mandir at Benaras and a temple at Gauhati and the Mahakali Mandir at Ujjain, large *Jagirs* for their maintenance and upkeep. On the other hand, while he destroyed Hindu temples he also broke down the Jama Masjid at Golkonda as he suspected a conspiracy against himself.

Indo-Islamic Architecture

One of the most fascinating aspects of Muslim history in India is the Indo-Islamic architecture. This is characterised by the adaptation of Indian resources, expertise, design, and motifs to the needs of Islam. The unique stalactite bracketing beneath the balconies of the tapering cylindrical Qutab Minar was executed by Hindu workmen. The horse shoe shape of the central opening of the 'Ala'i Darwaza was never imitated, but its grace and charm cannot be questioned. Tughlaq architecture, with its heavy, severe lines, influenced monuments in Malwa and the Deccan. Iranian curvilinear architecture is juxtaposed with traditional Hindu ornamentation in mosques at Cambay, Ahmedabad, and Champanir.[11]

Although Akbar deliberately chose to follow Hindu architectural styles, what emerged was an eclectic pattern. In the Fatehpur-Sikri palaces, Hindu imagination was superimposed on Iranian simplicity. The niches and windows give a unique lightness and airiness to Humayun's tomb. The kiosks, or *chatris*, at its corners make the mausoleum typically Indo-Islamic. The terraced structure of Akbar's tomb at Sikandra, near Agra, reminds one of Buddhist monuments. It seems that the imposing Panch Mahal (the five-storeyed palace) of Fatehpur-Sikri was transferred on to Sikandra in a new-form. The elegant mausoleum of Jehangir's father-in-law, Iltimadud-Daula, marks the transition from the pre-Shahjahan era to the phase of Shahjahan's imperial structures. It's delicate inlay work in hard stone, foreshadows the ornamentation of Shahjahan's monuments in Delhi and Agra. The elegance and majesty of the Taj Mahal, which Shahjahan built to immortalise his queen, Mumtaz Mahal, ensured its place as one of the wonders of the world; the imagination and sensitivity of its design made it the unparalled flowering of Indo-Islamic civilization.

The *mehrabs* of the Aurangzeb decorated Hindu shrines; and the Muslims whether Pathans, Arabs, Turk, Persian or Moghul likewise borrowed from the Hindu architecture in the making of their palaces and shrines.

The Mughal miniature was another important aspect of blossoming of Indo-Islamic civilisation. It offered an opportunity for the blending of influences from European figurative art, particularly Flemish and Belgian, with the art of the East.[12]

Before the rise of Islam, Indian merchants had settled in the Yemen, and the Jat population in the Persian Gulf ports was substantial. After the Arab conquest of Sind and the establishment of the Delhi Sultanate, a phenomenal expansion occurred in both maritime and overland trade and communication. The Delhi sultans exchanged gifts, luxuries, and novelties with West Asian and Central Asian courts. Muhammad bin Tughlaq sent Ibn Batuta as his envoy to China; horses from Arabia were exported to India from all the southern ports on the Persian Gulf and were bought by both Hindu rajas and Muslim sultans. The sultans and the Hindu rulers owned ships on the western coast of India, as did rich Hindu and Muslim merchants and the Mughal emperors and dignitaries.

Role of Women in Indian History

From the time of their earliest settlement, there were inter-caste marriages between Hindus and Muslims. For example, when Khwaja Muinud-Din Chishti settled at Ajmer he took two wives. One of them was a Sayyid's daughter, and the other was a Hindu *raja's* daughter who had been seized during a raid on the Hindus by the local Muslim commander. Sultan Alaud-Din Khilji married Kamla Devi, the widow of Raja Karan of Gujarat, who had been taken captive after the *Raja's* defeat.'[13] Alaud-Din's son, Khizr Khan, married Kamla Devi's daughter by Raja Karan, Deval Devi. During Alaud-Din's reign, Ghiyasud-Din Tughlaq, whom the Sultan had made Governor of Dipalpur, married his brother Rajab to one of *Raja* of Dipalpur's daughters. Firoz Shah Tughlaq was their son. During Muhammad bin Tughlaq's reign, Firoz himself married the pretty sister of Gujar, Saharan.[14]

It is significant that the Shaykhzadas (descendants of the Sufi leaders) married *Brahman* girls. In the sixteenth century Miran Sadr-i Jahan and Shaykh Abdur-Rahim, who hailed from Avadh, married *Brahman* wives whom they had obviously chosen themselves".[15]

Women played a significant historical role. Turkan Khatun,

Raziya's mother, was the most prominent among Iltutmish's queens. Qazi Minhaj was deeply impressed by her munificence to the 'Ulama, holy men, Sayyids, and Muslim ascetics. Raziya, herself not only commanded the army against rebel *iqtadars* but was also a brilliant administrator. Her successors were arch intriguers. Malika-i-Jahan, Sultan Nasiruddin's mother, was the principal instrument behind her son's rise to the throne. According to Ziauddin Barani, Jalaluddin's wife paved the way for 'Ala'uddin's accession by preventing her elder son from assuming his father's crown immediately after Jalaluddin's assassination. Ibn Batuta was deeply impressed by the generosity to the Sufis and Ulama of Makhduma-i Jahan, Muhammad bin Tughlaq's mother.

The ladies of the Mughal palace were proficient in both horsemanship and social etiquette and were also often astute politicians and artists. Akbar's mother, Hamida Banu Begum, was a capable adviser to both her husband and her son. Indeed, Humayun owed much of his success at Shah Tahmasp's court in Iran to her astute diplomacy. Akbar's wife, Salima Sultana Begum, was also endowed with superb mental powers and natural ability. The woman writer Gulbadan Begum has been immortalised by her facile pen, while Nur Jahan's role as the power behind Jahangir's throne need not be repeated here. Mumtaz Mahal, Shahjahan's wife, was the Emperor's leading counsellor, and after her death her place was taken by their daughter, Jahan Ara. Jahan Ara was also Dara Shikoh's principal supporter; but despite this, Aurangzeb took her into his confidence after Shahjahan's death.

Father Monserrate reported that the imperial *farmans* (royal decrees) were sealed, eight days after they were received from the *wazir*, by one of the queens, in whose keeping is the royal signet ring and also the great seal of the realm". The small signet ring (*uzuk*) was affixed to *farmans* granting senior appointments, titles, *jagirs*, and the payment of large sums of money. During Shahjahan's reign the *uzuk* was kept in Mumtaz Mahal's custody. On the queen's request it was handed over for some years to her father, Asaf Khan, the *Wakil*. After Mumtaz Mahal's death it was controlled by her daughter, Jahan Ara.[16]

The birth of a son was deemed a blessing by both Hindus and Muslims; girls were unwelcome. Although the Rajputs took many wives, they considered girl babies a curse, and female infanticide was widespread. Both Muslims and Hindus married off their children at an early age without their consent. Dowry was essential for girls and was a great strain on a family. Many Muslims with several daughters were full of praise for *sati* (the Hindu custom of incinerating widows on their husbands' funeral pyres). However, others, like Ibn Batuta, were shocked to see the enthusiasm at these *sati* scenes. Akbar's ordinance forbidding the forcible burning of Hindu widows was not strictly obeyed.

Aurangzeb's successors to the Mughal throne in the eighteenth and nineteenth centuries never changed their policies of peace and friendship with all religious communities. Religious polarisation did not take effect until the end of the nineteenth century, when competition for positions in the newly constituted British civil service was one of the major factors in exacerbating the differences which eventually led to the partition of India in 1947.

It should be noted that even though Hindus and Muslims followed different religions, their economic and political interests were the same. Even socially and culturally the

Hindu and Muslim masses as well as classes had developed common ways of life. A Bengali Muslim and a Bengali Hindu had much more in common than a Bengali Muslim and a Punjabi Muslim had. Moreover, Hindus and Muslims were being equally and jointly oppressed and exploited by British imperialism. Even Sayyid Ahmad Khan had said in 1884:

> Do you not inhabit the same land? Are you not burned and buried on the same soil? Do you not tread the same ground? Remember that the words Hindu and Musalman are only words of religious significance—otherwise all persons, whether Hindu or Musalman or Christians who reside in this country constitute one nation. When all these groups are called one nation, they should be one in the service of the country which is the country for a11.[17]

The Ulama and Muslim League

The two nation theory was contested by the *Burham*, an organ from the reformist 'ulama from Deoband. They indicted the Muslim League for its 'collosal blunder' which had no parallel in the history of Islam. "The verdict of history will go against a leadership which brought ruin and destruction to the community".[18] (*Burhan*, Delhi April 1948, p. 133). The question then arises; how could the communal and separatist trend of thinking grow among the Hindus and Muslims?

Although Azad's opposition to creation of Pakistan is well-known, the opposition by the other Ulama is not so well publicised. It is known only to the experts and scholars of the freedom movement. In fact the whole organisation of

Muslim divines called Jami'at-al-'Ulama-i-Hindi was a supporter of the Indian National Congress and never budged from its position even in the heyday of the clamour for Pakistan. In fact, most of the Ulama of Deoband and of the Jamiat al-Ulama joined forces with the Congress. In April 1940 the Jamiat sponsored an Azad Muslim Conference of nationalist Muslim parties such as the All India Muslim Majlis, Khudai Khidmatgar, Shia Political Conference, Majlis i-Islam, Momin Conference, Krishak Praja Party, and the Anjuman-i-Watan, which, in opposition to the Muslim League demand for a separate Muslim state, declared India as 'the common homeland of all its citizens irrespective of race and religion'. Representing at that time a substantial number of Indian Muslims, they assembled in Delhi to protest against the Pakistan idea and against the use made of the Muslims by the British government and others as an excuse for political inaction. Their views were summarised by Allah Bur Soomro, premier of Sind, and president of the conference, who said that to regard 'Muslims as a separate nation in India on the basis of their religion was un-Islamic'.[19]

Maulana Hussain Ahmad Madani, one of the most eminent Aalims from India, was another well known opponent of the idea of Pakistan while opposing the two-nation theory. In fact, according to him, the very spirit of the Qur'an is to encourage harmonious co-existence in a multi-cultural, multi-racial and multi-religious world. The Qur'an says, "For every one of you we appointed a law and a way. And if Allah had pleased He would have made you a single people, but that He might try you in what He gave you. So vie one with another in virtuous deeds". (5:48)

As soon as the two-nation theory resolution was passed on 23 March, 1940, Maulana Hussain Ahmad Madani undertook a whirlwind tour of India appealing to the Muslims not to be misled by the Muslim League's propaganda. The Maulana was attacked by the League hooligans who threw garbage on him.

Maulana Madani, Maulana Hifzur Rahman and other 'Ulama, fully supported the concept of *muttahida qaumiyyat* (composite nationalism). Moreover, they fully justified it on religious grounds. In this they cited the *sunnah* (practice) of the Holy Prophet. When the Prophet migrated from Mecca to Madina various religious communities like the Jews, Pagans and Muslims existed. These religious tribes and clans, had distinctive identities and traditions. The Prophet, therefore, drew up a charter (*mu'ahidah*) with the representatives of the religious communities and tribes and accorded them full freedom to practise their own religion.[20]

The 'Ulama, therefore, argued that when the Holy Prophet himself had set up a composite city-state in Madina why cannot we in India along with the Hindus and others accept the concept of composite nationalism. The only assurance asked by the 'Ulama from the Indian National Congress was that the Muslims could freely practise their religion in independent India. This assurance was readily given.

Recently Muslim scholars have brought to light that Hindus constitute a group of the "ahl-e-Kitab". Scholars from Hazrat Shah Waliullah, Maulana Sulaiman Nadvi and Maulana Obaidullah Sindhi to Maulana Shams Navaid Usmani, have contributed to this research. Though such findings have not "percolated down to the Muslim masses", scholars confirm that Hindus were the *Ummah* of Prophet Noah recognised as *Maha Nuwa*. "Evidence from the *Markandaya Puran* and several Vedas, and their description of *Jal Pralaya* (devastation caused by the flood) have been most helpful in this search."

"Beginning with the term *Dharma* and *Deen* (both meaning ways of life), and as an emphatic assertion of the Oneness of God (*Ekam Sat: La Ilaha Illallah*) Islam and Hinduism share the vision of a moral order prevailing in the universe. Both *dharmas* inform us of the cosmic agencies keeping an account of all our deeds for which we will be made accountable. Both talk about life after death..."[21] The orthodox from both communities, however, have inculcated distrust, created religious misconceptions and an inveterate hatred towards the "other". Ibn Batuta, after his travels through India, had, also observed that no Muslim was either allowed to enter the house of a Hindu or given food in the same vessels as theirs. He wrote, "If a Muslim is fed out of their vessels, they either break the vessels or give them away to the Muslims." On the other hand, Muslims were taught to look down upon idol worshipping Hindus and their caste system. The Sufi-Bhakti Movement, however, countered this faithless act and put their mite into uniting the two communities by overcoming such misconceptions.

Composite Traditions

Two great exponents of communal amity in northern India, Kabir (1444-1518), a weaver and Guru Nanak (1469-1539), the founder of Sikhism, through their writings and teachings, music and songs, emphasised human unity. One of the outcomes of the close interaction and free intermingling between the two communities was the birth of a common language known as *Khariboli* which later developed into Urdu. The flourish of the arts such as music and poetry during this period blossomed into a cultural and literary renaissance fostering inter-communal fusion. Rulers such as Zayn al-Abidin's in Kashmir (1420-70), the Husayn Shahi dynasty (1493-1539) in Bengal and the Bahaman's (1347-1526) in the Deccan, the Adil Shahi of Ahmadnagar (1490-1600), the Imamid Shaikhs of Berar (1485-1574), the Basid Shahi of Bidar (1492-1619) and the Qutub Shahi of Golconda (1512-1687) are watermarks of Hindu-Muslim fraternity.[23]

It is disheartening therefore, that the Yashpal Committee appointed by the Government of India, has recommended the omission of medieval history from the syllabus of school children. Deletions of periods from history can be as endangering as distortions and exaggerations since they create a hallway for speculation, suspicion, fundamentalism and cultural chauvinism.

K.R. Malkani's reference to Mahmud of Ghaznavi as "this master brigand was quite a secularist... his Indian coins were struck in Sanskrit and they bore the image of either Laxmi or Shiva's Nandi. He recruited not only Indian soldiers but also Indian commanders like Tilak, Sundar and Sewandram,"[24] and of Tipu Sultan as "Indeed the more I read of Tipu the more impressed I am with his rich personality. Young Tipu had two tutors, one Hindu, *Pandit* Govardhan and one Muslim, *Maulvi* Obaidullah. His life-long companion was Parnaiyya; his Commander-in-Chief was Krishna Rao; his private secretary was Shivaji. He had endowed 156 temples..."[25] are revealing observations.

There are several treatises on Hindus Muslim intermingling, cultural-social fusion of the communities on inter-community interest. These reveal an enlightened conception of both society and state grounded in fraternal relationship, symbiosis and traditions of religious tolerance. In his "*Lifting of the Veil*" from "*the gems of Islam*", Champak Rai Jain, a devout follower of Jainism wrote "To ascertain the truth about the teaching of Islam, and to separate its valuable gems from valueless stones as also from the glittering pebbles, so that its beauty may be brought out to public notice."[26]

An uncritical acceptance of colonial construction of Islam and the Muslims along with the inner religio-cultural tensions within a national paradigm, superficial intellectual probings shorn with rhetorics, and an inferior perspective of the 'other', unfortunately impressed that Islam had a rather crude approach to the problems of philosophy and metaphysics. Also, consequently there were no serious interpreters of Islam, no counterparts to Al-Beruni, Amir Khusrau, Malik Mohamad Jasi, Abul Fazal, Raskhan Rahim or Dara Shikoh. M.N. Roy disturbed by the fact that Hindus and Muslims having lived together for centuries did not learn to appreciate each other concluded that a deeper understanding "would shock the Hindus out of their arrogant self-satisfaction, and cure the narrow-mindedness of the Muslims by bringing them face to face with the faith they profess."[28]

A review of history shows that the Sufi-Bhakti movements struck a chord of harmony while many Sikh saints who are revered were not untouched by Sufi-Islamic teachings. Hazrat Mian Mir was invited by the fifth Sikh Guru, Arjan Dev, to lay the foundation of the Golden Temple. Raja Ram Mohan Roy, founder of the Brahmo Samaj, was also influenced by Rumi and Hafiz. Little is known of the temples, crematoriums and churches existing in several parts of Arabia, particularly in Dubai and Bahrain even today. It is time to accept that the history of the Muslims in India is not all violence or anecdotes of kings and lusty emperors but a spiritual, intellectual and artistic symbiosis as well.

In view of the continuing, communal hatred and violence

between the Hindus and the Muslims precipitating death and woe initiated mainly from living in a negative past, one is reminded of the words of Shelley on his reminiscence of the Trojan war:

Oh Cease! Must Hate and Death return?
Cease! Must men kill and die?
Cease! Drain not to its dregs the urn
Of bitter prophecy
The world is weary of the Past
Oh might it die or live at last!

Breakdown in relationships are not irretrievable. Such is the creation of people born in an unhappy age. The fragmentation of a society is lead by a dominant leadership which estranges the masses and tries to create a corresponding schism in the souls of people. People then loose their bearings and rush down blind alleys. However, greater souls can transfigure life by sowing the seeds of harmony.

The people of India, the Hindus and Muslims in particular, can generate a new consensus to avoid confrontation and create mutual trust and respect. It is time to rise like the phoenix from the ashes of the past and create a new temper to meet our national requirements and create a much needed stability.

It is only the mediocrities in civilisation who have disregarded the oneness of being and deeper experience. Would it then be wrong to say that the tyranny of politiking on critical issues has been the dividing line among people?

References

1. *Islamic Spirituality: Manifestations*, edited by Syyed Hossein Nasr, Crossroad, New York, 1991.

"Indo-Islamic spirituality and Literature", Annemarie Schimel, p. 262.

2. *Ibid.*, p. 262.
3. *Kitab fi tahqiq ma li'l Hind*, Al Beruni, Hyderabad 1958 (Arabic) English Translation E.C. Sachau, *Al Beruni's India*, (London 1887; Delhi 1965 reprint Vol. I), p. 31.
4. *Religious and Intellectual History of India in Akbar's Reign* by S.A.A. Rizvi, Delhi 1975, pp. 207-9.
5. *A History of Sufism in India*, 2 Vols., (Delhi, 1978, 1982), pp. 423-24.
6. *Shah Walliullah and his Times* by S.A.S. Rizvi, Canberra 1980, pp. 329-35.
7. *The Life and Works of Amir Khusrau* by W.M. Mirza, Calcutta, 1985, p. 143-44.
8. *A History of Sufism in India*, p. 254-56.
9. *Living Islam: From Samarkand to Stornoway*, Akbar Ahmed, Penguin Books, 1995, p. 218.
10. *Ibid.*, pp. 218-20.
11. *The Wonder that was India* by S.A.A. Rizvi, Vol. II, New Delhi, 1970, pp.278-303.
12. *Ibid.*, pp. 278-303.
13. *A History of Sufism in India*, Vol. 1, p. 124.
14. *Religious and Intellectual History of Muslims in Akbar's Reign*, pp. 183-84.
15. *Ibid.*, pp. 183-84.
16. *The Commentary of Father Monserrate*, translated and edited by Hoyand & S.N. Banerjee, London, 1922, p. 209.
17. *The Philosophy of Indian Nationalism* by R.C. Banerjee, (New Delhi, Concept Publishers, 1981), pp. 111.
18. *Legacy of a Divided Nation: India's Muslims since Independence*, Mushirul Hasan, (Oxford University Press, Delhi, 1997), p. 97.
19. *India's Partition: Process, Strategy and Mobilization*, edited by Mushirul Hasan, (Oxford University Press, Delhi, 1993), pp. 149-50.
20. *India's Partition: Preludes and Legacy*, edited by Ramakant Rajan Mahan, "*Freedom Struggle and Partition*" by Asghar Ali Engineer, Rawat Publications, New Delhi, pp. 176-91.
21. "Spiritual Symbiosis: Links between Hinduism and Islam", Sultan Shah in *Times of India*, July 28, 1988; p. 12.

22. *The Delhi Sultanate*, R.C. Majumdar, (Bombay, 1960), p. 132.
23. *The Widening Divide: An Insight into Hindu-Muslim Relations*, by Dr. Rafiq Zakaria, (Viking, 1995), pp. 8, 9.
24. *The Politics of Ayodhya & Hindu-Muslim Relations*, K.R. Malkani, (New Delhi, 1993), p. 76.
25. K.R. Malkani as quoted by *Muslim India*, June 1990, p. 280.
26. *The Lifting of the Veil from the Gems of Islam*, Champak Rai Jain (Bijnor Jain Parishad Publishing House, 1931).
27. *India and Europe : An Eassay in Understanding*, (Albany : State University of New York Press, 1988), Chapter 2.
28. M.N. Roy, *The Historical Role of Islam*, (Delhi, Indian Renaissance Institute, 1981), Reprint. Translated into Hindi by Chandrodaya Dixit.

Bibliography

1. Batley, C., *Indian Architecture*, (Bombay, 1965).
2. Brown, P., *Indian Architecture (Islamic Period)*, Bombay, 1975, 2nd rev. edn.
3. Briggs, Martins S., *Everyman's Concise Encyclopaedia of Architecture*, (London, 1959).
4. Fergusson, James, *History of Indian Art and Architecture*, 1876; (Delhi, 1967), reprint.
5. Havell, E.B., *Indian Architecture*, (London, 1919). *A Handbook of Agra and the Taj*, (Calcutta, 1924).
6. Archer, W.G., *Indian Miniatures*, (Greenwich, 1960).
7. Arnold, T.W., *Painting in Islam*, (London, 1928).

   and Wilkinson, J.V.S., The Library of Chester Beatty; *Catalogue of the Indian miniatures*, 3 vols., Bloomsbury, London, 1936.
8. Brown, P., *Indian Painting under the Mughals, A.D. 1550 to 1750*, (New York, 1975), reprint.
9. Clarke, C. Stanley, *Mughal Painting: The School of Jahangir*, (New Delhi, 1983).
10. Gershuis, M., *Indian Painting*, (London, 1978).
11. Gray, Basil, *Treasures of Indian Miniatures in the Bikaner Palace Collection*, (Oxford, 1951).
12. Arnold, T.W., *The Preaching of Islam*, (London, 1896).
13. Burkhardt, T., *An Introduction to Sufi Doctrine*, tr. D.M. Matheson,

14. Carpenter, J., *Theism in Medieval India.* (London, 1921; New Delhi. 1977). reprint.
15. Cunningham, J.D., *A History of the Sikhs*, ed. H.L.O. Garrett and R.R. Sethi, Delhi, 1955.
16. Gibb, H.A.R., *Mohammedanism*, (New York, 1958).
17. Halepota, A.J., *Philosophy of Shah Waliullah*, (Lahore, n.d.).
18. Houram, G.F., *Essays on Islamic Philosophy and Science*, (New York, 1975).
19. Husain, Y., *Glimpses of Medieval Indian Culture*, (Bombay, 1957).
20. Izutsu, T., *A Comparative Study of the Key Philosophical Concepts in Sufism and Taoism*, (Tokyo, 1966).
21. Mcleod, W., *Guru Nanak and the Sikh Religion*, (Oxford, 1968). 22. Mirza, M.W., *The Life and Works of Amir Khusrau*, (Calcutta, 1935).
23. Nicholson, R.H.A., *The Mystics of Islam*, (London, 1914).
24. Pearson, *Merchants and Rulers in Gujarat*, pp. 40-44, 76-77, 83-84, 93-95,
25. Qaisar, *The Indian Response to European Technology and Culture*, pp. 70-104.
26. Irfan Habib,'Usury in Medieval India', *Comparative Studies in Society and History* (The Hague), VI, 1964, p. 413.

India's Contribution to the Development of Islamic Sciences

Ahmed el-Sayed el-Heseasi

Since ancient times, India, a country rich in products' and its mythology, had been conquerors' target and a place of attraction for traders, tourists, seekers of knowledge and wisdom, and for religious preachers, poets and writers. They all crossed over to India through the passes on its north-western frontiers. Seldom were there those who came from its north-eastern side.

After much fighting, either they settled in this huge country or went back to their homes carrying with them, light in weight though precious in quality, wealth from India.

These outsiders whether they came as conquerors or tourists or as traders used to settle in India and enjoy welfare and prosperity and spiritual peace and tranquillity. Later they mixed with Indian people, lost their identity and constituted a group in Indian society.

Aryans, whether in their first advent (about 1500 BC) when they came as conquerors or in their second arrival (986-87 AD) led by Subtageen, his son Mahmood and all Ghaznavide rulers followed by Ghawrids, they all came with the message of Islam. With the spread of Islam, Islamic civilisation and Persian language in India, its history changed. Islam was the august gift Muslims offered to Indian populace and brought in them a change for better in the shadow of the revealed heavenly religion.

The advent of Aryans can be divided into two stages. The first stage was destructive like a flood because it brought destruction and killing. The second stage was marked by the establishment of a new civilisation and by the spreading of high culture. The first stage did not last long because it had no sound basis. But the impact of the second stage was far reaching historically, culturally and civilisationally. Sultan Mahmood Ghaznavi (387-421 AH) was able to take over a part of Punjab and some northern parts of India. But scholars like jurisprudents, philosophers, *Mohaddiseen*, Sufis, physicians, poets, writers and all kinds of Islamic theologians attracted the Indian people and led them with light and guidance. Indians even today have love in their hearts for them. Their services can never be separated from history, civilisation and culture of India.

The reasons why these people came to India were varied. Some of them came to spread Islam and guide people to welfare and prosperity while others came here to propagate knowledge and various sciences. Some of them visited India in search of knowledge and wisdom while others looked for fame, honour and wealth. Many of them joined the army or worked in government offices. Every group worked hard to spread Islamic belief and sciences in Indian society. Moreover, they learned Indian arts and sciences and translated their valuable books and wrote their commentaries whether the books were written in Sanskrit, or in any other regional language. They returned to their homes carrying the cultural wealth of India. Their scholarly contribution and valuable literary works were the ones that helped us to know the history, culture and civilisation of India.

Indian Kings care for Persian Poetry

Abdul Hai Hasani says:

> When Islam spread in India, it gathered Muslim writers from Khorasan. Their language was either Persian or Turkish. They spoke in their languages and made excellent contribution in writing and in composing poetry in Persian language. It became hereditary to their nature. Some of them even surpassed those who were born in Persia.
>
> The first person who composed poetry in Persian in India, was Sheikh Masood bin Sa'd bin Salman of Lahore. He was in the days of king Ibrahim bin Masood. He had many collections of poems. His poetry was popular and in circulation among people.[1]

Here, we concentrate upon the 10th century of Hijra i.e. 16th Century AD. Due to their love for literature and respect for Islamic culture, Indian kings welcomed poets from Iran. The hostile circumstances back home forced them to come to the courts of Indian kings. Ali Akbar Shihabi says:

> In the Safavid period the Iranian relations were expanded. Iran exchanged representatives and ambassadors with the countries that had no relations earlier with her. In respect of India, these relations were stronger than others politically and in literature.[2]

Syed Mohammad Raza says:

> The important aspects of Safavid period were the influence of the Persian language and literature, and its popularity in the neighbouring countries, especially in India which became the biggest centre for Persian poets.[3]

Edward Brown says:

> On the basis of Gibb's work, Jami, Amir Alisher Nawai, Urfi Shirazi, Faizi Dakani and Saib Asfahani — each one had influence on Ottoman poetry, and they became ideals for the writers. Ottoman critics wrote many letters of appreciation about these writers.

This and there are many other references that occur in the books of history of literature about the writers of this period and their travel in this huge Muslim country and the reciprocal impact between them and this country. The scholar should follow the pace of writers in this huge region and their movement in a bigger area of the world which, in addition to Iran, the centre of Safavid rule with its various provinces, included Transoxiana and India with all its states, including Iraq and Asia Minor or at least he should study the movement between Iran and India.

It is also necessary for the scholars not to look at the kings' courts where the poets used to earn their livelihood with their poetry depending upon the rewards and gifts from the rulers, princes and senior officials of the state. The scholar should go beyond and see the common environment in public functions, clubs and coffee houses which were the meeting points for poets and writers. These places were not less important than the royal courts since the coffee houses were open places for the writers and poets to compose various genres like elegy, satire, fun and jokes etc. which they could not express before kings, princes and rulers.

Poets from Iran

The scholar can also discover various forms of folk literature in these places which he may not find in the courts.

Perhaps the coming of writers, specially that of the poets to India can be considered one of the major and serious matters that appeared on the horizon of human relations in the Safavid society. In fact, one can not simply depend upon what is mentioned in the books of history of literature about this matter, its causes and consequences. Because whatever is written about their coming is basically the output of the care and concern Indian kings showed for poets and writers, and the rewards and gifts which they offered to them.

Shibli Nomani says:

> When the noble nature and generosity of the Taimoori kings became popular, India attracted poets from Iran.[4]

Syed Ali Raza Taqvi says:

> It should be noted that the Persian language and literature took on glamour in the Indian sub-continent since Akbar's era, the Persian literature and poetry improved and became unexpectedly very popular in this huge land, because the kings and princes encouraged it.[5]

Brown has given the reason for the travel of Iranian poets to India saying that it was wealth that brought them to

India. He has given examples from their poetry.

Ali Akbar Shihabi says:

> India became a centre for Persian literature and poetry and Iran was left behind in this regard.[6]

For that he gave reasons.

Taimoori kings in India had special interest in Persian language and literature. They were very active in giving countless rewards and prizes to the poets and writers of the Persian language by encouraging them and by bringing scholars and honoured people to India from far away countries.

In another place he says.

> Travel to India itself was a reward for Iranian poets and scholars. This has very clear reference in the poetry of the poets of that period.[7]

Therefore, who so ever could travel to India in that period, did not hesitate. But those who could not, they expressed in their poetry, their desire to travel to India.[8]

Tahiri Shihabi says:

> Indian Sultans and *Amers* encouraged a large number of poets from Iran to come to them. They never hesitated in giving them all kinds of rewards and prizes.[9]

Amiri Ferozi Gohi says:

> There was quite enough interest in Persian poetry and literature in the royal courts of Taimoori kings, their lords and leaders. The poets used to come to

> India hoping to get rewards and prizes. We seldom see an Irani poet who did not go to India, whether for a small period and get his share from that table of generosity.'[10]

But the scholar should not consider it the only reason for migration of poets and writers to India. The author of *Jame Mufeedi* narrates that when ready to travel to India, a close friend of his came to him and said. "What idea is this that you have thought of, and what is your intention? Perhaps you did not hear that the journey may claim human life. It is like a serpent that may kill people."

But the author was determined to travel insisting that travelling in the world removes the dust of sorrow from the surface of the heart. Man can see strange cities and different regions that may befill his heart with joy and may help him forget worldly concerns. And also because he does not feel comfortable with the high positions.[11]

This story stresses the point that the issue was not that of a desire for gifts or rewards but it was deeper than that. The scholar should have a look at the writings of the writers and the poets of that period to get the limits and results of this phenomenon clear in accordance with literature and the writers. Perhaps the first thing that a scholar notices is that the poets heard of the generosity of the Indian rulers and their encouragement to the poets and to poetry and their giving them big rewards and many gifts. Many of them did not hesitate to pack their bags to travel to India.

The poets who travelled to India used to face either success or failure. Some poets have expressed and mentioned about their success.

Encouraging the poets' travel to India, Zahoori says:

> If I were to explain the pleasures of being away from home, I would send people out of their homes. But I am not suffering from envy fever. If I stopped speaking about it, I am afraid that many sciences and people would be overlooked. I cannot deny its importance to this extent.

He says:

> Oh Zahoori! If you go to the homeland, I would bid you farewell, because I have become prisoner of this land, (India).

Sometimes, the poets used to suffer from total disappointment because of their failure in their travel to India. Therefore, in addition to the exertion of journey, the pain of homelessness was more, and the troubles of poverty, the pangs of remorse and the sorrow of failure increased.

Mohammad Qooli Saleem says:

> It was not our fortune to have our livelihood in the gardens of India. It was only a parrot that could understand our speech.

He again says:

> Oh Saleem! Have a corner in Kashmir and keep yourself away (from everything). It will be enough for you than going and coming to Agra and Lahore.

Although Abu Talib Kaleem was successful, but the success could come to him only after failing several times. He has expressed his failure in his words saying:

> Away from his home, there was none who was not happy I am appalled that the light is not equal to the lamp.

He says:

> I am imprisoned in the love of India, and ashamed of this journey which was of no use. Where is my bird of broken wings and the slaughtered going to reach?

Expressing his love for his homeland, the poet Mohammed Qooli says, "Oh Saleem! Ask whosoever travels from India to convey my regards to Iran.

Showket Bukharai says:

> There was nothing more than the darkness of being away from home. The dust of my homeland is like the light of zinc for my eyes. My stay has increased sorrow in my heart while I came out of my home clear and clear like that of a mirror.

He says, "I composed this poem in India while the initial lines were composed in Iran. Oh Saleem! The days became excited because of my words."

He says, "From the humiliation in my homeland I came to the life of a vagabond. So either have mercy upon me or allow me to travel."

Impact of Poets' Migration

Putting aside the poets' opinions about their travel to India, there should be some non-negligible impacts of this migration phenomenon.

Perhaps the first impact of this migration was the reference to this new country with its various regions, in a way that never was there in Persian literature. Because such a large number of writers from Iran had never travelled to India, even in Ghaznawid era.

It was natural that they were fascinated by this new environment, with its natural beauty, ample benefits and a new hope for name, fame and wealth. In the following we will give some examples from the poetry of this period where India is depicted with its different regions.

Abu Talib Kaleem says:

> Bad omen is away from India, the country of happiness. The heart is here responsive and the nature very fluent. India is the Qibla of the region of good health, vitality, and the mirage is also full here with nectar.

It was natural that the poets spoke of the rituals, traditions and rites that were prevalent in that area, and the characteristics, deeds and the festivals of Indian people in order to get mixed in the environment and live with the people there. Abu Talib Kaleem says about the festivals of India:

> The days became beautiful like a garden because of these two festivals. The eye of happiness is shining like the eye of the bowl of wine. The happiness is our companion in the temples of heart. The sun of happiness is lighted with these two lamps. The festival of King's sitting on the throne and that of his weighing have become one. The heart is sitting high on the peak of happiness.

Mohammad Qooli Saleem says describing a *Brahmin* girl of India:

> I saw a *Brahmin* girl in a temple, the head of the idol bent down for her when she bowed her head (because the idol was fascinated with her beauty).

He says:

> Oh Saleem! One can not ignore the beauty of brown skinned women. My heart did not see in Kashmir what it saw in India.

Kaleem says:

> The religious obligations were so popular in India that the thirsty land did not drink water in the month of fasting.

Coming to India resulted in many references to journey and its suffering, being away from home and its pains and love for ones' own land.

Mohammad Qooli Saleem says:

> Your love made me home away from home and changed the desert into garden in my eyes.

He says:

> I knew no home because of my mad love. When there was desert, I did not know the society. Since it took me very long time to return from the journey like that of a griffin, therefore I knew none of my countrymen.

He says:

> What is the difference between home and being away from home, because the pain of your love made me a stranger among the known ones.

He says:

> Oh Saleem! Till when should I change the dust of Geelan into clay because of my crying in love of my friends from Iraq.

Talib Amli says:

> Oh Talib! When a breath from the garden of Iran came to me, my heart felt inclination towards Tooran.

On his way to India, Talib Amli visited the city of Qandhar, but left it soon, only to return there after he travelled to a number of places in India. He got in touch with Eatimadul Dawla, the minister of the emperor Jahangir. Through him, he reached the royal court. Eatimadul Dawla in his lifetime appointed him as "*Mehrdar*". But this high post could not suit his poetical nature. Therefore, after a brief period, he sought his leave and left.

Talib Amli joined Sufi cults in Lahore. He was the follower of Sheikh Abdul Ma'ali. He himself has mentioned it in his poetry.

He married in 1025 or 1026 AH, when the queen herself mediated to choose his bride. Of this marriage, two daughters were born, the elder was called "Kalan" and the younger "Khurd". His eldest sister, Sittun-Nisa Begum took care of both of them until they were married.

Talib Amli was elevated in the royal court of Sultan Jahangir.

He reached up to the post of "King of the poets". It was in the year 1028. This is also mentioned by Jahangir in his book "Tozak Jahangir".

At the last stage of his life, Talib chose loneliness. Because he believed that loneliness is the basic thing. Therefore, some people accused him of madness. He died in 1236 AH.

It is easy to differentiate between Talib's style in Iran from that of his in India. We find that Talib used difficult and out of use words in his poetry in Iran. He exaggerated much in using allusions and metaphors. But when he went to India, he brushed up his talent and kept himself away from using difficult words. His style was known for the fluency and eloquence preserving the Persian language. He rarely used Indian terms and phrases. If we find some of them, it is because there was no alternative in Persian. Showkat Bukharai says:

> Oh my lord! How can I pay my debts to you. I have become attached to you and I am away from my home.[12]

In the end, it becomes very clear, how India contributed at that period of time in enriching and developing the Islamic literature. It was because the Kings and Sultans of India encouraged the writers who migrated to India. They were encouraged by care and a great deal of kindness which they received from them.

References

1. Abdul Hai Hasani - "*All-Thaqafatul Islamia Fil Hind*" edited by Abul Hasan Ali Hasan Nadwi, (Damascus 1983), p. 328.
2. Ali Akbar Shihabi - *Rawabit Adabi Iran wa Hind*, p. 68.

3. Syed Mohammad Riza - *Tareekh Adabbiyat Iran*, p. 267.
4. Shibli Nomani - *Shirul Ajam*, Vol. 3, p. 3.
5. Syed Ali Raza Taqvi - *Tazkira Naweea Der Hind wa Pakisan*, p. 86.
6. Ali Akbar Shihabi - *Rawabit Adabi Iran wa Hind*, p. 34.
7. *Ibid.*, p. 39.
8. *Ibid.*, p. 40.
9. Tahiri Shihabi - *Muqaddama Diwan Talib Amli*, p.24.
10. Amiri Feroz Gohi - *Muqaddama Diwan Saib Tabrezi*, p.4.
11. Mohammad Mufeed Mustawfi *Qazweeni* - *Jame Mufeedi*, pp. 767, 776.
12. Dr. Mohammad el Sayed Abdul Momin - *Al-Zawahir el-Adabia Fil Asr el-Safawi*, pp. 65-76, (Cairo, 1978 A.D.).

Translated by Dr. M. Ayub Nadwi

India's Contribution to Arabic Literature

S. Ziaul Hasan Nadwi

India's contribution to Arabic literature is so vast and wide a field that it can not be covered in such a thin paper.

However, Arabic language has been an area of interest for Indians since the advent of Islam. This language was the only medium of conversation and exchange with Arab traders frequently visiting the coastal cities of India. Mappillas of Malabar in south west region of India can hardly conceal their Arab origin. Gujarat, Maharashtra, Karnataka and Kerala have been famous centres where Arab traders used to come and stay according to their will.

The local population under their rulers accorded hearty welcome to these loving guests. These contacts and cordial relations had made the atmosphere very congenial and friendly for them. Thus Arabic language, culture and literature "no longer remained an alien field of knowledge to India and Indians. Islam which entered this part of the world through Arab traders attracted the local population very much. People started embracing Islam individually in the beginning and collectively at some places afterwards. A sizeable number of these new entrants got more and more curious for Islamic sciences. Arabic language being the only key to open the locks of this vast treasure of light and learning won its share from their attention. This resulted in invaluable works in the form of commentaries on *Holy Quran*, *Hadis* literature, *Fiqh* literature, *i.e.* jurisprudence, *Tasawwuf* or Islamic mysticism and ethics, theology, philosophy, historical literature, astronomy, medicine and philology and literary compositions.

Works on India in the Arabic Language

There are many Indian words used by Arab traders who borrowed these words from Indian languages, like *sandal, misk, kafoor* and *karanful, filfil, hair, zanjabil, narjeel, jayphal, lemon, tambool*, etc. The word 'Hindi' was added to some Arabic words as adjective like '*Ood-Hindi*', '*Kusht-Hindi*', '*Tamare-Hindi*'. In the same way, Arabs are indebted to Indians for Indian numericals which are known as *Al-Arqamul Hindia* till today. Another major contribution of India to Arabic literature is astronomical material. The book *Sind-Hind* attracted the attention of the Arabs in the second century of *Hijra* and was translated by Al-Faradi in 770 AD. It was once again translated by Mohammad bin Musa Khawarlzml. Al-Beruni also wrote a book on the subject with the title *Jawami-ulmaujood'li Khawatiril Hunud fi Hisabat tanjim*. Abu Bakr Razi wrote a book in the field of medicine in 932. Ibne Nadim has given about 15 names of Indian authors whose works had been translated into Arabic. Two story books *Kalila-wa-Dimna* and *Alf-Laila-wa-Laila* are also from Indian origin. The game of chess which plays an important role in Arabic literature and Arab society is also an Indian contribution. The word *Shatranj* is taken from the Sanskrit word *Chaturanga.* Al-Beruni's *KitabuI-Hind* may be regarded as a very great contribution of India because it is full of knowledge and learning about India which Al-Beruni had written and presented to the world of learning.

Qur'anic Commentaries from India

Commentaries on Qur'an have the first and foremost important place in Islamic literature. Only a few names will be mentioned here. For example, *Tafseerur-Rehman-wa-Tayseer al-Mannan* written by Alauddin Ali bin-Ahmad Mahayami in 1431, *Al-Tafseer al-Mohammadi* by Sheikh Mohammad bin Ahmad Miyanji bin Nasiral-Din Gujarati in 1547, *Tafseer-e-Mazhari* by Qazi Sanaullah Panipati in 1810, *Shu'-unal Munazzalat* by Ali Muttaqi Burhanpuri in 1568 and *Tarjamat al-Kitab* by Muhibbullah Allahabadi in 1648, *AI-Tafseeraatul Ahmadiyyah* by Ahmad Bin Abu-Sayeed in 1717, *Fath-al-Khabir bima Labudda min hifzihi Fi ilm al-tafseer* by Shah Waliullah Dehlavi in 1702, then Abdul Haq Muhaddis Dehlavi in the field of *Hadis, Lam'āt al-tanqīh 'ala Mishkāt al-Masābih,* Abul Hasan Sindhi's *Hāshiyah 'ala al-Bukhari,* then *AI-Musawwa* written by Shah Waliullah, on the famous book of *Hadis Muwatta Imam Malik* as its commentary. Then *Sharh Tarijim Abwābul Bukhari* by the same author. There is a commentary of *AI-Mawa-hibul Latifa* commentary on *Musnad Abu Hanifa.* Here is a dictionary of *Hadis* known as *Majma' bihar al anwar fi ghara'ib al-tanzil wa Lata'if al-akhbar* by Mohammad bin Tahir Patani. In the field of *Fiqh* i.e. Islamic jurisprudence, a lot of work has been done. In India Shah Waliullah has written *Al-lnsaaf fi bayan sabab al-lkhtilaf.* He has also written *'Iqdul jeed fi Ahkam al-Ijtehad wat taqleed.* Then on the principles of *fiqh*, Mohibbullah Behari has written *Musallamus Suboot* in the age of Aurangzeb in 1717.

Books on Fatawa from India

There are five famous collections of *Fatawa* also. They are *Al-Fatawa al-Hammadiyyah* by Abul Fath Rukn bin Husamuddin, *Fatawa Ibrahim Shahiyyah* by Shihabuddin Ahmad bin Mohammad, *Fatawa Majma' ul-Barakat* by Mufti Abul Barakat, *Fatawa al-Tatar Khaniyyah* by Alim bin Ala'ul Hanafi Andapathi and the most famous of these *fatawa is Fatawa 'Alamgiri* which is known in the Arab world as *Al-Fataẇ-al-Hindia* also. It would not be out of place here to mention some other books also like *Zubdatul Ahkām fi Ikhtitaf a'immatil 'Alām* in the field of *Fiqh*. Then *Al-Manasiku-s-Saghi*r by Rehmatullah bin Abdullah Al-Sindhi. The book *Fara'idul Islam* by Mohammad Hashim bin Abdul Ghafoor Sindhi, *Jam'i-u-Ta'ziraat* which is a collection of penal code by Chiraguddin Ali Alqazi. In the field of *Tasawwuf*, *Al-Qaulal Jameel fi Bayani Sawais Sabeel* by Qazi Sanaullah Panipati, *Irshadul Talibeen* by Abdul Karim Mohammad and there are many other books.

Works on Sufism

Then on the methods and practices of Sufism there is *Al-Jawaharul Khamsa* originally in Persian and rendered into Arabic by Sibghatullah Gujarati. Then *Al-Risala fi suluk Khulasati s-Sādatil Naqshbnndiyyatis Siddiqiyyah* by Tajuddin Zakaria. Shahabuddin Daulatabadi has written in the field of Arabic grammar *Irshadul Nahwa*. In the area of lexicography, there is a famous book '*Al-Obabuz Zakhir* by Hasan Sagani. Very large number of synonym words in Arabic, have been recorded in *Kitabul Azdad* and *Kitabul Zeb.* For instance there are more than 21 words for 'light', 52 words for 'darkness', 29 words for the 'sun', 88 for 'wealth', 350 for the 'lion' or 'tiger', 100 words for 'camel', 255 words for 'she-camel'. The book *Kitabul Zeb* contains almost all Arabic words for the wolf. Majduddin Ferozabadi has written a famous dictionary *Qamoos.* Then *Muntakhabul Lugh-at* was also written as a commentary on *Al-Qamoos.* On the subject of rhetoric and prosody, Ghulam Ali Azad Bilgrami mentioned in his *Subhatul Marjan fi Asar Hindustan* that the ancient Hindus invented many figures of speech and rhetoric devices, common between them and the Arabs. In the field of literary composition, prose and poetry, oratory and correspondence literature, India has contributed volumes. Some famous names of poets and prose writers are Ghulam Ali Azad Bilgrami, Faizul Hasan Saharanpuri, Maulana Zulfiqar Ali Deobandi and Maulana Aizaz Ali as poets; Mulla Mahmood Jaunpuri, Shah Waliullah Dehlvi as prose writers. There are famous literary selections in the prose known as *Nafhutul Yaman fis ma Yazulu bi Zikrihi al-Shajan* by Ahmad Mohammad Al-Yamani. Mohammad Husain Khan of Shahjahanpur has written *Riyazul Firdaus.* And Abul Faiz Faizi has written *Mawarid al-Kilam wa Silk Durar al-Hikam.* These are all books of Arabic prose.

Then *Maqāmātul Hindia* was written by Sayyid Abul Bakr bin Mohsin al-Alawi and *Al-Manaqib al-Haydariyyah* written by Ahmad bin Mohammad Yamani by order from Ghazi al Din Haydar, the king of Oudh. There are scores of commentaries and glossaries on standard classical literary works written by Indian writers before independence. Those who won great name and fame in the 20th century in the field of Arabic language and literature are Nawab Siddiq Hasan Khan of Bhopal. There are more than 30 Arabic books to his credit. Maulana Hakim Syed Abdul Hai Hasani who wrote an encyclopaedic book in the name of *Nuzhatul Khwatir wa Bahjatul Masām'i wa Nawazir* in eight volumes. This book has been reprinted with the name of *AI-Elam biman fil Hind minal Aalam* by his able son and author of many books, Maulana Syed Abul Hasan Ali Hasani. Another prominent name in this field, is the name of Abdul Aziz al-maimani who has frequently been recognised by Arab scholars. Then other names are— Shaikhul Hadis Maulana Zakaria, Abdul Hai Firangi Mahali and Maulana Syed Sulaiman Nadwi, who has written *Siratun Nabi*, biography of the Prophet in six volumes, and Shibli Nomani and Hamiddudin Farahi.

Maulana Syed Abul Hasan Ali Nadwi's book *Māza Khasiral Alam binhitat al-Muslimeen* is the history of decline and fall of the Muslims and the impact it left on the world civilisation. This is a very famous and popular book. There is an interesting story that Maulana Abul Hasan Nadwi wrote this book when he was 35 years old and this valuable book was included in the library of Al-Azhar. After some years, he visited Al-Azhar University and requested its librarian that the same book may be given to him for consultation. He was denied on the pretext that the book was rare and written by a very famous Indian writer. So it cannot be issued. Instead he was advised to read it in the library. Then after the intervention of the university rector, the book was issued to him. And the author was introduced to the librarian who apologised for the inconvenience to Maulana Nadwi.

There are many great institutions like Nadwatul 'Ulema, Darul' Uloom Deoband, Madrasatul Islah, and in South India Darul Salam, Umarabad. All these great institutions have contributed a lot and they have very rich libraries telling themselves the importance of Indian contribution to Arabic literature.

Index